EXPERIENCE and GOD

EXPERIENCE and GOD

by

JOHN E. SMITH

Fordham University Press
New York
1995

LC 95-31950
ISBN 8232-1624-1 (hardbound)
ISBN 8232-1625-x (paperbound)
ISSN 1073-2764

American Philosophy Series, No. 3
Vincent M. Colapietro, Editor
Vincent G. Potter (1929–1994), Founding Editor

Library of Congress Cataloging-in-Publication Data

Smith, John Edwin.
Experience and God / John E. Smith.
p. cm.—(American philosophy series ; no. 3)
Includes bibliographical references and index.
ISBN 0-8232-1624-1 (hardcover).—ISBN 0-8232-1625-X (pbk.)
1. Religion—Philosophy. 2. Experience (Religion) 3. God.
I. Title. II. Series.
BL51.S573 1995
291.4′2—dc20 95-31950
CIP

Printed in the United States of America

FOR

Reinhold Niebuhr

THEOLOGIAN, PROPHET, TEACHER, FRIEND

Contents

Acknowledgments, ix

Preface to the New Edition, xi

Introduction, 3

I. The Recovery of Experience, 21

II. The Religious Dimension of Experience and the Idea of God, 46

III. The Disclosure of God and Positive Religion, 68

IV. Doubt and Living Reason, 99

V. The Argument about God, 121

VI. Experience, Community, and the World Religions, 158

Epilogue: Religion and Secularization, 180

Index, 207

Acknowledgments

No one can succeed in acknowledging all of his intellectual indebtedness, largely because it is impossible to draw up an accurate account. I want, nevertheless, to express my appreciation to students and colleagues at Yale for providing a community of conversation within which many of the ideas expressed in this book were first tried out. I want also to acknowledge with gratitude a research grant from the American Council of Learned Societies which helped to make possible an extended stay in London during which time I was associated with King's College at the University of London. Portions of my discussion of the world religions in Chapter VI were delivered as a public lecture sponsored by the Department of the History and Philosophy of Religion at King's College in 1965. These same portions have been previously published as an article, "The Structure of Religion," in the inaugural issue of *Religious Studies*, edited by H. D. Lewis; I should like to thank the Cambridge University Press for permission to use this article.

I am grateful for the encouragement and assistance of Wilbur Ruggles of the Oxford University Press and for the most helpful editorial advice of Miss Caroline Taylor. Many thanks are due to Mrs. Alan Slatter for her untiring efforts in typing the manuscript and in checking the proof.

Finally, I am indebted most of all to my wife, Marilyn, for her incisive criticism and indispensable correction of previous drafts of the pages that follow.

New Haven, Conn. JOHN E. SMITH
January 1968

Preface to the New Edition

The reissuing of *Experience and God*, a book written more than twenty-five years ago, provides a welcome opportunity to review some of the topics I discussed at that time. If, as Hegel said, philosophy is simply thinking things over, I have availed myself of the opportunity to think some of them over again. The text reproduced here is the same as the original published in 1968, and, while I shall single out some points about which I have new thoughts, I want to reaffirm the substance of what I wrote previously, especially the experiential approach to understanding and interpreting the significance of religion in human life.

In the Introduction to the previous edition, I called attention to the mutual involvement of religion and philosophy both as a matter of principle because of their overlap of interest and as a matter of history because of the long interplay between them during the course of Western civilization. I also took note of the unfortunate consequences suffered by both forms when they are divorced from each other. Without the goad of the ultimate questions that are the concern of religion, philosophers tend to set aside the metaphysical counterparts of these questions, and reduce philosophy to analysis and criticism, which often means the theory of knowledge. When, on the other side, religious thinkers reject philosophical discipline as something alien, they are often on the way to positivizing religious doctrine and to confining themselves to a closed sphere of faith so that the ancient quest for intelligibility—faith seeking understanding—is abandoned. The demonstrated truth is that no serious and constructive dialogue between philosophy and religion is possible when philosophy loses its metaphysical dimension and becomes purely critical or when religion becomes fundamentalistic and refuses to engage in any exchange.

The situation of three decades ago well illustrated the separation I have just described; in the intervening years there has been no radical change. With the important exceptions of the phenomenologists, those developing the legacy of the classical American philosophers, most Catholic philosophers, and the followers of Whitehead, the main philosophical stream is still analytic and critical. The old positivism, it is true, is no longer in force, having been dealt a serious blow by Wittgenstein, who redirected the discussion with his claim that the focus should not be on the "meaning" of expressions but on their "use" in the language of a community. The change was clearly for the better since religious utterances could no longer be ruled out in advance as meaningless. On the negative side, however, was the ensuing *fideism* that denied "rationality" to religious insight; in fact, in one pronouncement Wittgenstein went so far as to claim that if there were a scrap of evidence in behalf of a statement, it could not be a religious utterance. Wittgenstein's thought has been very influential among Protestant thinkers because it allows for the free expression of biblical ideas and presents no metaphysical challenge. Moreover, the prospects for the sort of philosophico-religious dialogue I have been arguing for have been given another blow by the anti–intellectualism of the religious right with its unphilosophical confusion of the Bible with a scientific treatise. We have, nevertheless, good reason to hope that the entire situation may be changed by the spread of the conception of experience developed by Royce, Peirce, James, Dewey, and others in opposition to what the British empiricists understood by "experience." From the new vantage point, science, morality, religion, art, philosophy are not closed spheres or realms confronting each other, but different contexts and dimensions of integral experience understood as the cumulative and meaningful outcome of all the encounters between ourselves and what there is.

Accordingly, my concern has been to construe the nature of experience in terms of what actual experiencing shows itself to be. This means among other things a major overhaul of the main tenets of modern "empiricism." There are several deficiencies in the view of experience bequeathed to us by Locke and Hume. Two are of major importance: first, the identification of experience with the data of the senses, and, second, the placing of our intellectual powers, our powers to understand and interpret experience, in a separate compartment under the heading of "Reason." From the first error comes the denial of meaning to any term for which there is no corresponding sense impression; from the second comes the result that "experience" becomes mute—sheer fact—because its articulation and interpretation are not internal to experience but descend upon it from the outside. On the classical view, the one who experiences is merely a passive spectator recording facts rather than a concrete subject actively engaged in living a life and in interpreting the events he or she undergoes in accordance with their interests and purposes. I concluded that, if the classical theory of experience were correct, much that everyone actually experiences falls outside "experience" altogether. This consequence seemed to me especially unfortunate in the case of religion, not only because

God is certainly no object of the senses, but also in view of the importance to religion of complex experiences suffused with a dominant quality such as awe in the face of the holy, gratitude in forgiveness, humility in repentance, and many others. I argued that if much that is experienced has to be denied or declared "merely subjective" because of a theory, it is time to get rid of the theory in order to preserve the experience.

For a resolution I turned to the broad and deep reconstruction of the meaning of experience set forth by Peirce, Royce, James, Whitehead, and Dewey. Experience in their sense allows ample room both for religious expression and for understanding its relations to other dimensions of experience. I have the distinct impression, however, that, for a large number of philosophers, after three-quarters of a century or more, the new view has not yet replaced the older empiricism. The neglect of the classical American thinkers is one reason; the other is no doubt the fact that the thinkers cited above were critical of what many philosophers at present hold dear, namely, a professional view of the field and a belief that epistemology should continue to be at the center of discussion. Be that as it may, I am convinced that one can make no sense of the experiences vital to religion if experience is what it was said to be by Locke and Hume.

I continue to stress the point that I find it more adequate to speak of a religious dimension of experience (by which I mean a context defined by a person's concern for and allegiance to an object of unconditional devotion) than of "religious experience." I have given a number of reasons in the text for my misgivings about this concept; among them is the way the idea may be misused. I noticed while reading a recent textbook outlining arguments for the existence of God that there has been added to the already familiar arguments the "argument from religious experience," which turns out to be an attempt to derive a divine existence from the fact of "religious experience." Such an idea totally misunderstands not only the nature of experience but its place in religion as well. Experience is encounter with what there is; experience is made up of what we undergo and live through, and its meaning becomes part of the integrated life of a person. Experience is not a datum to be looked at by a spectator; nor is it a fact to be used as the basis for an inference to its supposed cause. I find it instructive that Dewey, for whom religion was not a central concern, nevertheless rejected this sort of approach in *A Common Faith*, and for much the same reasons I give.

If I were asked to single out the most important change in my present views as compared with those expressed in the text, I would point to some new ideas stemming from my attempts to relate in some fruitful way the two different approaches to God represented by the Ontological Argument, on the one hand, and the cosmological arguments, on the other. My interest in the topic was first kindled by Paul Tillich's paper "The Two Types of the Philosophy of Religion" published in 1946 and reprinted in his book *The Theology of Culture* (1959). I regard this as one of the most illuminating essays I have ever read, but I had not discovered it by the time I was writing *Experience and God.* The paper is an exposition of the two great traditions in Christian thought in the period that stretches from Augustine to Aquinas: one is the meditative quest for illumination and the recovery of the presence of the Uncreated Light in the depths of the soul, first set forth by Augustine and later formulated as the Ontological Argument by Anselm; and the other is the approach to God through the world, inspired by the thought of Aristotle and brought to a culmination in the now familiar cosmological arguments for the existence of God set forth by Aquinas. Several years ago, I had the good fortune to be asked to take part in "Conversations" with Fr. W. Norris Clarke on the occasion of his Suárez Lecture at Fordham University. I presented a paper, "The Two Journeys to the Divine Presence," in which I called attention to Tillich's essay and the impact it had on my thinking about the arguments for God.[1]

I believe Tillich was right in bringing to light the basic differences between the quest for God through the soul which we find in Augustine, Anselm, the Victorines, and Bonaventure, and the approach of Aquinas which starts with the world and moves to God via the principle of causality. There is, moreover, a decided tension between these two approaches as can be seen in the fact that, in preparing the way for beginning with what is better known to us—that is, the world—Aquinas set the Ontological Argument aside, declared that the intelligible principles of *Sapientia* are no "closer" to God than the sensible species since both belong to the created intellect, and claimed that, while the existence of Truth in general is self-evident, the existence of a Primal Truth is not evident to us. My purpose here is not to join the issue of the superiority of one approach over the other, but rather to direct attention to the possibility that they may be coordinated in some way since it seems that we need both because of their different starting points, each way doing something that the other does not. I am thinking here of the truth in Peirce's rejection of the chain conception of deductive argument—the chain is only as strong as its weakest link—and his adoption instead of the rope analogy—many strands of argument tending in the same direction join together in mutual support. Tillich proposed to subordinate the cosmological way to the ontological, but I was not entirely satisfied with that solution and I kept wondering whether there might be some unifying link between them. I believe there is and that it is to be found in the idea of *presence*.

For a long time the major stumbling block to accepting the

[1] See *The Universe as Journey*, ed. Gerald A. McCool, S.J. (New York: Fordham University Press, 1988), pp. 131–50; see also pp. 170–77 for Fr. Clarke's comments. This discussion can serve as a supplement to my comments above, since I am unable to repeat here the contents of my essay.

cosmological way was the thought that causal inference always means a logical move from a reality *present*, in this case, the world, to a reality *absent*, that is, God. The outcome of the argument is a "must be" God who seems at least to stand in contrast with an "is" God whom we in some sense meet. My sense of this contrast was heightened when I discovered two passages in Anselm's *Proslogion* (chaps. 14, 16) in which he is perplexed by having found God but still having no experience of Him. "Why, O Lord God, does my soul not experience You if it has found You?" and, again, "You are within me and around me and I do not have any experience of You." Anselm has the sense that the certainty of understanding with which he grasps the necessity of the God who "must be" still falls short of an apprehension of presence, an encounter, the *hic et nunc* of the divine presence.

Anselm's experience led me to see that, different as the ontological and cosmological arguments are, each arrives at a form of rational *necessity*—the God who must be—and that reaching God through an argument must in both cases leave one with a sense of incompleteness that is overcome only through a stronger experience of presence. Presence became the key word for me and it led me in turn to reconsider the nature and place of inference in experience. From the pragmatists I learned that since experience is not an instantaneous affair but a temporal process, it must be understood as containing inference within itself. If this is so, inference need not be thought of exclusively as a move to what is *absent*, but can be taken to mean the directing of the mind from a present reality to *another present* reality inherent in the same reality from which thought set out. With this idea in mind, I returned to the two ways of approaching God and asked why they should not be understood as connected by the common goal of reaching the divine presence, albeit it in different ways. Hence, my figure, drawn from Bonaventure, of the two "journeys." In the ontological way the presence is in the Truth and the Light; in the cosmological way it is a presence in the cosmos. It is, however, precisely because the presence is not situated in the same way for the two approaches that the nature of the causal principle in the cosmological journey needs to be reinterpreted. The presence of God in the Light and Truth was not understood as a causal inference by any of the thinkers who followed this route. The world, however, as a spatio-temporal existence (and the same holds true for its other special constituents singled out in the cosmological proofs) can manifest the divine presence in its own being as nature, but the main emphasis falls on its contingency and the fact that it is not self-supporting but requires a Power beyond itself. Nevertheless, the causal inference involved to God as First Cause, etc., can be construed as a move from the world as present, not to an absent God, but to the presence of God in the world.

However, it then becomes necessary to understand causality in the rich sense it had in the thought of Aristotle, which means that thinking in terms of efficient cause alone is too abstract because it does not do justice to the ways in which the divine presence is manifest in the world. This defect can be overcome by going back to what used to be called "formal" cause with the emphasis on the ingredience of the *nature* of the cause in what it effects. The notion of efficient cause coupled with the relation of antecedent and consequent is inadequate because of its implication of a two-event situation where the consequent "follows" its antecedent, while the latter appears to be over and done with as something in the past, whereas what we want to insist upon is that this so-called antecedent is *present in* that consequence. The doctrine of continuous creation nicely expresses this point; as a one-event situation, the cause is contemporary with its product and is therefore not "over" when the product comes to pass. Or, to put it the other way around, were the continuous creativity to cease, the world would sink into nothingness.

In proposing to overcome my misgivings about the inference to the absent God in the cosmological arguments by finding the quest for the divine presence in both approaches, I do not mean to say that the differences between the two journeys disappear or are of no account. That would be an error, because the nature of any medium of divine disclosure enters essentially into what and how much disclosure that medium is capable of bearing or expressing. Not all features of God can be expressed through the world; indeed, if we had not already learned this lesson from the Christian tradition, it is clearly demonstrated by the Deism of the Enlightenment which was based on nature alone. The result was that—given the universe of Newton—God had to be conceived solely as a divine Mechanic. We know, however, that the person and the soul are more adequate vehicles of divine disclosure than the world of nature is, and it is on this account that we need to retain the approach to God represented by the Augustinian tradition and not suppose that it was permanently replaced by the Thomist synthesis. Self and world both are valid starting points for the religious quest; one moves inside and the other outside, but the goal of the two is the same.

I believe that my Epilogue about religion and secularization expresses much that is still relevant in the present situation. In the intervening years there has been a migration of the sacred in the form of what I call quasi-religions or secular substitutes for religions proper—Humanism, Marxism, Nationalism in many forms, together with a proliferation of cults inspired by charismatic figures. In all these cases some finite and conditioned reality—humanity, the state, the dialectic of history, the cult leader—has been elevated to the status of an absolute that demands the unqualified loyalty that biblical religion reserves to God alone. More often than not, those most attracted to quasi-religions are people who have come to experience a void caused by their disaffection with the religion in which they were raised or by the emptiness of a purely secular existence. They are vulnerable because they do not perceive the specter of the *demonic*—the sacred in its negative and evil guise—or the idol that so readily fills the void left by the loss of God. It is paradoxical that the awesome strength of the human need that religion answers is most clearly shown in the tragic failure of a cult or charismatic figure. I believe that Paul Tillich was right when he declared that the encounter of the world religions with each other is less important at present than the encounter each religion is now undergoing with the quasi-religions that have grown up in their midst.

There is one egregious shortcoming in the book and for which I do apologize, and that is the unrelieved use of "man" and "men." This is a practice not to be excused by the absence of any intention to exclude women. The long-established habit of understanding "man" and "mankind" to mean all human beings and certainly not males alone leads one to overlook the fact that, intentions notwithstanding, the usage is justifiably objectionable.

New Haven, Connecticut JOHN E. SMITH

EXPERIENCE and GOD

Introduction

Religion, described by a modern philosopher as "that region in which all the enigmas of the world are solved," has itself become an enigma for modern man. In former ages men struggled with the solutions offered by religious faith, accepting or rejecting them with some passion and concern; in recent decades the prevailing attitude has been chiefly one of indifference. For many people religion is not something to be condemned as false; it is regarded instead as outworn or dead. No better evidence for this conclusion could be cited than the various attempts that have been made to show the superfluous character of religious faith in a scientific age, or the numerous reductive interpretations that have been offered according to which belief in God is a purely human projection made by men who have lost their nerve. We have witnessed, moreover, the concerted efforts of so-called humanists to sever "values" from religion on the ground that moral ideals cannot be preserved if they are made to rest on a decaying foundation. But it is one thing to deal positively with the problems in human life with which religion proposes to deal; it is quite another to ignore them in the belief that the religious outlook is no longer a live option.

Two factors have played major roles in bringing about this state of affairs. One is a widespread failure of understanding what the religious dimension of life is and means; the other is a failure, largely on the part of theologians and religious people, to keep pace with the dominant thought patterns of the modern world. Among otherwise intelligent people one often hears the most incredibly naïve statements made about religion, its past history, and its present forms. And among avowedly religious people one often hears statements that indicate ignorance of the modern world, its political and social institutions, its technological organization, and the basic intellectual framework that determines the thinking of the secular mind. This failure of understanding and loss of mutual communication can be overcome only through radical reflection and self-criticism. An impasse in thought calls for further thought, and ultimately for a return to the experience that is at the base of all thought. In the present instance this means a reconsideration of the nature of religion, its place in the total structure of human life, and its relations to the secular culture in which the man of faith must live. This task is largely of a philosophical nature, not only because it is necessary to understand religion in relation to a comprehensive scheme of things, but also because the idea of religious truth is involved and the problem of truth in religion is intimately connected with the issues of metaphysics. Philosophy and religion have in fact always been involved with each other, especially in Western civilization, where the Judeo-Christian tradition took on its systematic theological form in response to the challenge of the Greek philosophical schools.

In the long period that extended from the days of the Fathers of the Greek Church to the high point of the Middle Ages, a continual dialogue took place in which philosophical ideas and categories were used for the expression of religious belief and the founding of theological systems. The thought of St. Augustine represents the finest product of that dialogue in the ancient world. So skillfully did Augustine interweave philosophical and theological conceptions that it is possible only with the greatest difficulty to say where one leaves off and the other begins. The Augustinian approach maintained itself for centuries until changing historical circumstances forced it into the background. The development away from Augustinianism culminated in the great *Summae* of Thomas Aquinas, based on a different statement of the relation between theology and philosophy. The solution of Aquinas depended on the idea of a division of labor and the marking out of proper spheres of concern and competence for the two disciplines. Revealed theology was to be responsible for the clear and systematic presentation of the content of revealed truth, and philosophy was to be confined to the rational analysis and interpretation of all existence, its kinds and levels. Whatever problems were solved by Aquinas' definitive separation of philosophy and theology—and there is no denying the element of truth in his masterful synthesis—new problems were created. The fact that Aquinas, following the lead of Aristotle, thought primarily in terms of hierarchy and levels of reality caused him to establish an hierarchical relation between theology and philosophy, so that he envisaged theology as the final wisdom that stands beyond and completes the knowledge that is philosophy. Each discipline was to enjoy autonomy in its own proper sphere, and the fact of their common source in God, in Truth itself, meant that they could not conflict; nevertheless, it is doubtful that the hierarchical conception can allow for a critical dialogue between the two. One result of this failure was the gradual widening of the gap between philosophical thought and theological expression. And, as has been pointed out repeatedly, if Aquinas freed philosophy from the domination of theology, philosophy came to free itself still further only to become, in the end, the handmaid of the new mathematical science.

The present situation shows the final outworking of the divorce between the intellectual enterprises. Due to loss of confidence in the power of reason to deal with speculative problems, and the spectacular success of experimental science, philosophy has been reduced to analysis and critical clarification. Instead of interpreting the significance of scientific knowledge for human life, many philosophers have tried to imitate the scientific approach, and in the process have restricted philosophy to the clarification of what is presumed known from other sources and on other grounds. One result has been the decline of comprehensive interpretations of man and the world which might serve as critical counterparts of theological systems. A genuine and important encounter between theology and philosophy is possible when philosophy is represented by constructive interpretation: for example, Augustine viewed the Christian faith in relation to the comprehensive outlook of Plato and the Neoplatonists, and Aquinas set Christianity off against the equally comprehensive vision of all things to be found in Aristotle. But such an encounter fails or becomes oblique when philosophy is represented *only* by critical thought, by semantics, semiotics, logic, and linguistic analysis. It is not that these topics are unimportant; it is rather that no genuine, creative, and critical discussion is possible when theology is represented by definite answers to certain questions—the existence of God, the nature of man, the doctrine of salvation—and when philosophy offers nothing substantial on these topics but is represented instead by critical discussion of preliminary questions such as how such questions can be answered, what language is to be used, etc. Under these circumstances the dialogue becomes oblique or is transformed merely into the "analysis" of religious language.

It is no accident that modern theological thought has been able to find a point of contact with philosophy only in two cases—existentialism and process philosophy. And the reason is not difficult to discover: the existentialists and the followers of Whitehead have been attempting to deal from the philosophical side with at least some of the problems to which theology is addressed. The Christian doctrine of man, for instance, can be critically and fruitfully compared with the understanding of man set forth by the philosophers of existence, and the Christian idea of God can be compared with Whitehead's theory of God as primordial and consequent. Such comparisons are essential for keeping the philosophical accounts in contact with religious insight and for bringing to bear on theological thought the critical perspective of philosophical analysis. But no such comparisons are possible when philosophers are not dealing with the speculative problems directly, but come armed instead merely with critical apparatus and ground rules, so to speak, that are to determine the framework within which any critical discussion can take place. In the case of critical philosophies, the implicit metaphysics buried in them has to be developed and made manifest before a critical dialogue can take place. Two different answers can be critically compared only when they are intended to be answers to the same question. Nothing more than an oblique and preliminary discussion can take place when a theological answer is met, not with a philosophical answer, but with semantical rules or theories about the general structure of language and its uses. The situation, moreover, is further complicated by the fact that, in many instances, the restriction of philosophy to critical questions is part of a more comprehensive intention to avoid the speculative questions entirely or to prevent them from arising in the first place on the ground that such questions are illegitimate and stem merely from the "bewitchment" of intelligence by the corrupting influence of language.

The disastrous consequences of the divorce between philosophy and theology—to be seen most clearly in the resurgence of purely fideistic theology on one side and purely critical or second intentional philosophy on the other—can be overcome only if a relevant encounter can take place. One way in which this may happen is if religious thought once again becomes what it has been so many times in the past, namely, a goad to philosophy, driving the philosophers to focus their attention on at least some of the comprehensive and speculative problems, and if theologians take seriously their unavoidable involvement in the use of philosophical categories and in the presupposition of philosophical doctrines. If each perspective is thus essentially involved in the other we may hope that philosophical thinking will be turned once again from the consideration of purely critical questions to the direct confrontation of first order questions and that theology will be forced out of its purely confessional enclosure to face in a rational way the philosophical alternatives that challenge religious doctrine. The ultimate aim is to overcome the emptiness and formality of philosophy and to frustrate the obscurantist and parochial tendencies in theology.

Every attempt to consider religion in philosophical perspective is presented at the outset with a host of difficulties, not the least of which is the frequently expressed suspicion that the term "religion" does not denote any identifiable subject matter at all. Full-scale treatment of these difficulties will be given in the course of the argument; several points, however, are so basic that they must be mentioned at once. From a nominalistic standpoint it is illegitimate to speak about religion in generic terms, on the ground that, while there may be a "family resemblance" between the different religious traditions, we should properly bound our statements, confining them to an identifiable religion such as Christianity or Buddhism, and avoid the supposition of an "essential nature" definitive of religion as such. From the standpoint of a theological particularism it is also illegitimate to speak about "Religion" because to do so is said to involve us in a generalized and purely human "religiosity" with which a positive faith such as Christianity is likely to be confused. Avoidance of this confusion is the main motive behind the frequently expressed claim that Christianity is *not* a religion in the sense that it is one more member of a class made up of the many historical religions. Some theologians have claimed that because of the *sui generis* character of Christianity it cannot be understood within any general framework that might also be used for interpreting the non-Christian religions.

If these claims go unchallenged, a philosophical treatment of religion becomes impossible. But must we accept these claims? That religion in general or *überhaupt* does not confront us as an historical reality may be admitted at once; the point must even be insisted upon. That only individual or identifiable religious traditions can be said to have historical form, however, does not prove that there is no such thing as a *religious dimension* in human existence, nor does it prove that religions fail to have a generic structure that can be defined and illustrated. If a multitude of religions is admitted—and there are none but pedantic reasons for denying such a multitude—then some basis must be found for denoting them by the same term. There is no contradiction involved in the claim that a set of phenomena can have a definite structure without that structure itself having a separate existence. It is possible to show that there is a religious dimension to human existence and also that the historical religions do have a common structure without also claiming that either the dimension or the structure exists by itself. Nor is it necessary to speak as though the religious dimension were itself a religion, and certainly there is no need to regard the defining of such a dimension as the attempt to construct a "natural" religion or a substitute for any historical religion. A philosophical interpretation seeks to understand religion, not to create it.

Theological nominalism may say that whatever has a generic nature or belongs to a kind cannot be unique, but there is no necessity that this should be so. In fact it is only when a phenomenon is identified as being of a certain kind that we are in a position to show wherein its uniqueness is found. Of the absolutely unique it is likely that we can say nothing whatever. Perhaps the difficulty results from the confusion of the unique with the final or ultimate. Those who say that Christianity does not form merely one "religious" answer among others, and seek to express the point by saying that Christianity is unique, are guilty of confusion. What they mean is that the Christian answer is the final or ultimate answer for them, and that, in comparison with that answer, the faith and doctrine of other religions simply do not count. But if this is what is meant, then calling Christianity unique is misguided. If there are several answers to a problem and one of them is regarded as final or ultimate by me it is not necessary to express this claim by saying that the others are not answers at all. To be final or ultimate is not the same as to be entirely beyond classification.

There is a further problem stemming from the interweaving of universal and particular in the phenomenon of religion: it concerns the fact that the philosophical treatment of religion is always carried out not only from a particular philosophical standpoint, but also within the framework of a particular, historical religion. This means that, in the present case, the religious outlook of the Judeo-Christian tradition will play a more important role than will any other recognized religion; yet this need not confine the argument to Christianity alone. There are two principal reasons for the limitation of outlook; both belong to the nature of the situation in which all thinking takes place. First, it is a plain fact that every thinker exists in a situation where some one or another of the recognized religious traditions has been decisive in shaping his thought. Every thinker, therefore, is related either as believer, critic, or, if this attitude is possible, mere observer, to the religion that has been decisive for himself and his culture. No pretensions to being a "free-thinker" or a cosmopolitan intellect changes this fact. Even if a person should claim to be free of all religious commitment and attempt to confront the multitude of religions as if it were a matter of freedom and autonomy to choose one or reject them all, the fact would remain that the person would already have been shaped to some extent and, indeed, decisively related to one of the historical religions. Even if I should view it as a live option to become a Buddhist or to become a convert to Islam, it would still remain the case that I had been decisively related to the religious tradition of my native culture—the Judeo-Christian tradition. Second, since religion in its generic form does not have separate historical existence, the results of a philosophical account of religion would lose their point and import unless they were related to a particular religion. We must take both factors together; on the one hand, the thinker by nature finds himself unable to transcend the decisive religious tradition of his situation, and on the other, it is important that he seek consciously to show the special significance of what is true about religion generically for the particular religion to which he is related. Only in this way will it be possible to do justice to the fact that all actual religion has individual, historical shape and also to the further consideration that no religion is at all intelligible apart from an understanding of the structure of human life in the world. Despite the uniqueness and finality to which all particular religions lay claim, the fact remains that no one of them is independent of those universal conditions in human life that make religion possible (and, ultimately, necessary) in the first instance.

It is often said by theologians that an analysis starting with the universal fact of religion involves us in a morass of subjectivity and forces us to depend entirely upon purely human experience. It has now become a commonplace even among religious thinkers to speak disparagingly of "religion" and to make light of so-called religious experience. The suppositions behind such a view are twofold: it is supposed, first, that reflection on the nature of religion as a universal phenomenon in human life must lead to an avoidance of God and of transcendence in favor of purely human responses, and second, that this, in turn, reveals the acceptance of the view that "experience" is no more than feeling or subjectivity and hence is insufficient for expressing the claim to truth and objectivity that accompanies serious religious faith.

There are good reasons for regarding these two suppositions as mistaken. Moreover, those who persist in such views are damaging the cause of religion in the modern world; they make it difficult, if not impossible, to explain what religion means and why it is inescapable, and they are forced to abandon experience because they are too willing to accept an outmoded conception of what it is and means. In the face of these errors it is of the utmost importance to show that there is a religious dimension to human existence and that this dimension is unintelligible without reference to God or transcendent Being. The philosophical standpoint required for this task is that of a radical empiricism, making central the doctrine that experience is an objective and critical product of the intersection between reality in all its aspects on the one hand and a self-conscious being capable of receiving that reality through significant form on the other. In short, the major task is to show that religion without God is impossible, and that experience, so essential for religion, need not be conceived as a tissue of subjectivity but is rather the medium of an objective encounter with the real world.

Despite much talk of "empiricism" in modern philosophy, actual experience in its full range and depth has frequently been ignored by philosophers in favor of tailor-made and truncated versions of experience that have been fashioned to suit some special need. More often than not, experience has not been consulted for what it actually does disclose; instead it has been used merely to illustrate foregone conclusions about what it *must* reveal if it is to meet the requirements of some rationalist program. Experience has suffered not only from the stigma of being subjective in the sense of being unreliable as a guide or standard, but it has been hedged in by various types of *a priori* demands. Concentration upon language, upon the forms of expression, upon experience only after it has been well formed and articulated, has frequently had the effect of filtering out of the rich content of primary experience only what can be expressed in some conventional language. Expression is, of course, essential and can be transcended entirely only if the pure immediacy of which mystics speak is a reality. But it is illegitimate to conclude from the necessity for expression that one can adequately approach experience solely through that channel. Analysis of the *general* structure of expression, whether it be the rich categorical analysis of Kant or the much more restricted analysis offered by linguistic philosophers, can never be more than the anticipation of the formal features of experience. A more radical return to experience in the full range of encounter is demanded. Analysis of the general shape of expression does not reach the singular experience and all that it contains. Experience, then, needs to be rescued not only from the charge of subjectivity, but also from the restrictive force of approaching it only through expression, that is, only through language. Instead of trying to fit all experience into a pre-existent language, we must attend to the more difficult matter of finding the proper language in which to express all that we experience. Experience drives toward expression, which is why the finding of adequate language is a genuinely creative task; but there is no corresponding drive in the opposite direction. When our language proves inadequate, we return to experience, but we do so in order to criticize our language and improve it, not to force our experience into conformity with a pre-established language.

The bearing of the foregoing on the interpretation of religion must be made clear. The basic roots of religion in experience can be understood only if experience is seen as an encounter with an objective world in the dual sense that the encounter is something objective and that what is encountered at the same time transcends the subjectivity of the individual and of any finite collection of individuals. The reason behind the choice of this term for the description of experience is that it best expresses the fact that in experience we *find* something already there, we *come up against* something, we *confront* persons, objects, events, and we do so with the sense that we *undergo* or receive whatever it is that we meet without any sense of being responsible for having produced it. Encounter, however, is minimal; in encounter we do not pass beyond the surface or "face" of the object. Encounter is the beginning of experience but not its end. Every item encountered has a "depth" as well as a surface, and the penetration of this depth requires various inter-actions between ourselves and what we encounter, whether these operations be intellectual or physical. If, for example, we see a circle drawn on a page, we encounter it as a line with a curvature which we call "round," but at that stage we have not yet penetrated to its depth, which includes such facts as that this figure is one which encloses a maximum area for a given perimeter, or that it constitutes a special case of another set of figures called ellipses. These interesting mathematical data belong to the depth of the circle and, while the circle encountered actually includes all these mathematical facts, these facts themselves are not encountered as such, but must be sought after, discovered, through processes of analysis. Religion must involve the experience of God, and such encounter is not to be thought of merely in terms of purely human feelings. If the experience of tables and chairs, of persons and communities, is not to be dissolved into a tissue of feelings, then neither is the experience of God. Moreover, a proper understanding of experience in all its dimensions of meaning will make it possible to show forth the religious dimension and especially to point out the manner in which the question of God necessarily arises in human life and reflection as a result of man's encounter with the world, with himself, and with other human persons. It will be necessary to point out the distinctively religious aspect of the question of God and show how this aspect is related to God as understood from the reflective standpoint. For there is a philosophical as well as a religious aspect to God, and the two, though intimately related, must not be confused. Failure to understand the peculiar relation between the philosophical and the religious has led in turn to at least two erroneous views. On the one hand, there are those who suppose that philosophical considerations are irrelevant for understanding God in the religious sense; on the other, there are those who assume that it is possible to speak of God in some purely philosophical sense that has no connection whatever with religion.

The founding of religion upon experience leads to at least two further basic problems. The first is that of providing experience with critical support. The idea of a "pure experience" that is entirely self-supporting or self-authenticating can be no more than a limiting concept, pointing to what is never realized in fact. Experience stands in need of interpretation; moreover, it gives rise to differing views as to what is encountered and how it is to be interpreted. Therefore, some form of critical dialectic is unavoidable. The second problem confronting an experiential approach to religion is posed by the fact that actual religion requires particular, historical shape and that in the course of human history a multitude of such particular religions has emerged. Each has made revelatory claims or claims to authority and finality and each has expressed its historical belief in the form of definite doctrines. How are we to choose between them?

With regard to the first problem, it is important to show that while experience or encounter in religion can never be dispensed with in the sense that we can find some purely rational or conceptual surrogates that would make the experiential aspect superfluous, there is nevertheless the need to provide experience with rational support. It must receive, first, the *indirect* support that comes from showing such experience to be a trustworthy source of knowledge, and second. the *direct* support of a rational dialectic that makes it clear that the experience of God is intelligible. If the question be put whether providing experience with such support results in "proving" the existence of God, the answer is affirmative if it is understood as the claim that the unreality of God means at the same time the unintelligibility of all experience and all existence.

With regard to the second problem, it must be admitted that approaching God through the medium of the religious dimension of experience taken as a universal feature of human existence appears to conflict with the special experiences that are the foundation of the positive religions. Insofar as the religious dimension is described as a universal, structural feature of human experience and existence, it must seem that there is no logical route from that dimension to the singular apprehensions of God connected with special revelatory claims. The difficulty here is actually less formidable than it at first appears. Since the religious dimension is not itself positive religion, but the philosophical reflection of what religion is and means in human life, there is no problem of making a "transition" from this dimension to the particular religions and certainly no need to suppose that the numerous religions could in any way be "generated" by some logical process starting with the religious dimension universally understood. The positive religions, with their differences in doctrine and practice stemming from their differences in religious insight, represent different resolutions of the basic problem that becomes explicit in the religious dimension of experience—the problem of God as the ground and goal of all existence. But precisely because the problem is basic and universal there must be a *concept* of God or of a divine reality; the problem of God is not confined uniquely to any one historical religion. For if the term "God" is taken exclusively as a name denoting a reality to be believed in and worshipped only from within the limits of one religion, then, of course, it follows that no one outside of that religion can mean, refer to, or be concerned about "God" in that sense. The question, however, is whether it is correct to restrict the meaning of the term "God" in such a way that it becomes impossible to acknowledge the existence of a *general* problem concerning a divine Being. The problem of God and its solution cannot be merely a cultural affair, such that if I happen to live in one part of the world or to have been shaped by one particular religion I must confront this problem, but that if I happen to live in another part of the world I am free from it. There may be and doubtless are problems of this sort, but the problem of God cannot be one of them.

Moreover, it is precisely because the different religions, Buddhism, Christianity, Judaism, Islam, represent different responses and solutions to the same basic problem of God confronting man as man wherever he may exist, that it is possible and fruitful to compare these different religions and consider the question of their adequacy *vis à vis* each other. What makes the encounter of the world religions of special interest and importance is not the obvious differences in belief and practice they exhibit, but the possibility that these different beliefs all relate to the same problem—the problem of God as ground and goal of all existence. In view of the continuity of human experience in so many other areas, it is unreasonable on the face of it to suppose that there is no concept of and therefore no universal problem of God, and that only Christians face the problem, while Buddhists, for example, do not.

Further light on the problems raised by the particularity represented in each of the major religions in the world can be gained from considering the structure of religion, not as it appears in the direct experience of the individual—the main focus of the discussion about the religious dimension—but as it is exhibited in the corporate form of religion expressed through the religious community and the tradition to which such community gives rise. It can be shown that religion has such a universal structure wherever it appears and that this structure makes it possible to have a genuine encounter between the world religions. No experience regarded as unique within any religion need be sacrificed in the process; on the contrary, comparison with relevant alternatives can provide each tradition with a clearer understanding of itself and its own peculiar religious insight.

Finally, in view of the omnipresence of the religious community in the history of religion, it is essential to arrive at a proper understanding of the relation between the individual and the community as it concerns religious faith. The common assumption that religion in its social or community form represents merely "organized" religion in contrast with a purely individual (and therefore "real" or "genuine") piety, needs to be re-examined. And it especially needs to be re-examined by American Protestantism, for which individualism has long been a sacred cow. The emphasis on "conversion" as a purely private and personal affair, plus suspicion of the church as an institution, have had much to do with the failure of Protestantism to find a viable form of *religious* community. It is no accident that when many Protestant denominations come together for the purpose of establishing a corporate form in which the churches can effectively confront the many problems of modern societies, the only available models they find are nonreligious institutions, the bureaucracy of the state or the executive hierarchy of the modern business corporation. The nominalistic outlook that leads to an exaggerated individualism in many regions of modern life has also infected religion in America, with the consequent loss of a proper regard for the bonds that transcend the lonely individual and bring him into a community of suffering, of joy, and of faith. The fact that wherever we look among the monuments and records of religious traditions we are brought face to face with communities of some kind suggests that community can be neither external nor accidental.

On the other hand, however, there is no dimension of human life that is more intensely individual and personal than religion; no man can believe for another man, no man can confess for or be judged in place of his neighbor. How are these two factors to be related? How are we to understand the coming together of the most intensely individual and the most intimately interpersonal forms of life? The answer is to be found in sensing the deficiency of purely isolated existence and in the discovery that even before God no man can be entirely alone; a community is essential for faith no less than for life.

If religion is not to be discarded as a relic of the past and if the insight that it provides is not to be lost to a generation much in need of a wisdom that inquiry alone will not provide, a new understanding of what religion is and means is essential. The first step in the attainment of such a goal is the recovery of experience from the various distortions to which it has fallen prey in the modern world. With experience established in its proper place, the next step is the marking out of the religious dimension or mode of experience through which the problem of God first emerges. The dual character of this problem must be clarified so that the interconnection of philosophical reflection and religious faith will be seen as rooted in the nature of God and of human experience. *God is in one perspective a religious solution and a philosophical problem, and in another a philosophical solution and a religious problem.* The contexts differ, but the mutual involvement of the two dimensions is no accident; that involvement is made possible by the fact that God is at once the final purpose of life in its movement toward self-realization and also the final *Logos* or intelligibility of all being marking the end of the rational quest. Problem and solution are found on each side; as final *Logos*, God is the final solution to the philosophical drive of man toward understanding the totality of things, and within the same philosophical dimension the reality of such a self-dependent Being constitutes a final problem for reason. Within the religious dimension, God is the final solution for the longing of the self to pass beyond anxiety, guilt, and the threat of an empty existence; but God is also the final problem, in that the way of redemption is neither easy nor transparent, and it passes through a vale of self-sacrifice that must often appear not so much the fulfillment of the self as its annihilation.

From the emergence of the idea of God in human experience the next step is to understand the contributions of historical occasions to special insights and apprehensions of what God means and to their uniting force in establishing positive religious traditions. The connection between these historical occasions and the claims of revelation associated with them on one side, and the general or recurrent occasions that bear witness to God on the other, remains a problem to be solved. This problem is basic because it introduces the perplexing issues raised by the existence of a multiplicity of religions and conflicting claims to finality. These difficulties would remain insoluble were it not for the fact that religion has a generic structure that makes it possible to understand the world religions within the framework of a universal problem of God.

Finally, the vigorous and often uninformed hostility that exists in the modern world against organized religion, so-called, can be placed in a more critical perspective through a proper understanding of the religious community and the role it plays in the religious life. As a result, all simple oppositions between individual and community will be seen as misguided and in need of correction. Religion is more than the individual in his "solitariness."

Religion, like philosophy and its problems, is inexhaustible; critical reflection, no matter how comprehensive, cannot encompass the whole. Moreover, the actual situation helps to sift the different aspects of faith, marking out some for immediate concern and placing others in the background. In the modern world religion as a total dimension in human life has become a problem. It is as if one could not get down to the serious consideration of specific issues because of a general skepticism covering the entire subject. But that skepticism is so frequently based on ignorance and misunderstanding that it becomes necessary to confront it directly with a fresh interpretation rooted in experience and critical reflection. It will never be possible in the end to argue and by sheer force of reason to settle a person in a religious faith. The ultimate roots lie deeper. But understanding has its own role to play and it is a role played by no other power in human life. It removes the sense of the strange and the untrustworthy, of the one-sided and the explicitly irrational. The major step in the recovery of God in the modern world will be taken when religion no longer appears to us as something foreign, embarrassing, and outworn, but rather as the ultimate fulfillment of human existence. Beyond preliminary concerns that touch but a part of life is the final concern that focuses itself on the whole. The partial problems of life we may avoid, with greater or less success, but the problem of God we do not avoid.

I

The Recovery of Experience

The major intellectual task of the present is the recovery of experience from the distortions to which it has been subjected, and the development of a theory of experience that will express adequately its nature and proper place in the total scheme of things. The appeal to experience, the claim that what we think and say is supported by what we actually find, is not a novelty. The appeal is to be found in Aristotle and it appeared in a most powerful and decisive form during the period of the Enlightenment, especially in the writings of the classical British empiricists Locke and Hume. Moreover, the concern for experience and the demand that all thinking be based on what we actually find or encounter has been central to the development of American philosophical thought as represented by Peirce, James, and Dewey. A lesson of singular importance is to be learned from noticing that, while every appeal to experience is an invitation to consider what is revealed in our actual encounter with the world, all so-called empirical philosophies do not understand the nature of experience in the same way. It is not simply that there are different ways of describing and interpreting what we find, though these differences also exist, but that no appeal to experience is naïve, for every such appeal carries with it a *theory* of experience, some principle indicating what experience is and how much it is supposed to contain. Aristotle, Locke, and Dewey were all in some sense "empiricists" and yet they are not in agreement on the status experience is to enjoy or what it can legitimately deliver.

The most immediate response to the problem here indicated is to refer it back to experience for solution. Experience itself must be the touchstone; experience must present and define itself. Unfortunately this solution will not do; it is too naïve and uncritical. If the appeal to experience always involves, either implicitly or explicitly, the use of a principle of selection specifying what is to count as an experience, then there will be no possibility of a naïve appeal to experience to adjust conflicting theories of experience. The only possible procedure is to indicate at the outset what theory of experience is adopted and then discover by critical comparison and reflection whether it is more or less adequate than other theories.

The fact that we cannot approach experience uncritically and that a problem is raised by the existence of different theories of experience has an important bearing on the interpretation of religion. It is possible to understand experience in such a way that the rooting of religion in experience is precluded at the outset. There have been, for example, narrow theories of experience that would confine it to the data supposedly disclosed through the senses, with the result that whatever fails to meet the qualifications of being a sensible datum is *ipso facto* excluded from experience. Furthermore, experience has in the past been understood as the passive reception of what is "given" to a purely theoretical observer and the content of experience has been thus restricted to atomic data exclusive of relations, of tendencies, and of dimensions of meaning such as the aesthetic, the moral, and the religious. If such theories of what experience is and means are true it is pointless at the start to look for the foundations of religion in experience. But if the appeal to experience is never naïve from a philosophical standpoint and a theory of experience is unavoidable, the first step must be to give an account of experience that will be adequate for expressing all that we actually encounter and undergo.

The chief obstacles that have hindered the development of an adequate theory of experience in modern philosophy are these: First, many philosophers have assumed that experience is a "mental" product or a subjective deposit of feeling located within the consciousness of an individual. Second, many have assumed that language or a medium of expression are indispensable for the having of experience, and thus that it is possible to approach experience and apprehend its content by analyzing well-formed language. And as a corollary of the second assumption, there is the further supposition that it is sufficient—usually on the ground that thereby the utmost clarity is attained—to concentrate on but one language or use of language, either that of natural science or of logic. The first assumption has had the force of discrediting experience as a reliable channel of discovery concerning both the world and the human persons in it; the second assumption (and its corollary) has had the consequence that experience is restricted to theoretical knowledge and is regarded as revealing no more than what our most precise language has already expressed. In the first case it is the *status* of experience that is called in question; in the second the issue turns on the *nature* of experience. In either case the fundamental assumptions regarding experience must be examined.

In the most basic sense, experience is the many-sided product of complex encounters between what there is and a being capable of undergoing, enduring, taking note of, responding to, and expressing it. As a product, experience is a result of an ongoing process that takes time and has a temporal structure. Within experience there may be moments of apprehension or insight that seem to compress the process into an instant or pure present, so that they appear as "timeless" or "instantaneous." Whether this is in fact the case is not for present purposes as important as the fact that experience involves a process, and even if there are seemingly timeless moments in it, these will still take place within an ongoing stream that is temporal in character. Although experience is possible only for beings capable of response and expression, there is no need to identify the locus of experience uniquely within the being who has it. The main point of stressing the fact that experience is a product is to emphasize the co-operation of factors involved. The chief error of taking experience as "mental" or subjective consists in the uncritical assumption that experience is a record or report to be found entirely within the mind, consciousness, or feeling of an individual being. As soon as this assumption is made, the next step is the contrast between the so-called mental content and the external world as a public or objective collection of things. The final result is that objectivity, in the sense of what is stable, reliable, and independent of individual prejudice, comes to be attached to the so-called external world—while experience is taken as a merely subjective content. If, instead of thus prejudicing the nature of experience at the outset, experience were to be understood as a product of the intersection of something encountered and a being capable of having the encounter, apprehending it, and feeling itself in the encounter, and capable of interpreting the results, the need to assign the labels "subjective" and "objective" uniquely to one side or the other would vanish. The resulting experience, moreover, would not have to be located entirely within the consciousness or the mind of the being who has had the encounter, for that once again involves neglecting the fact that experience is the product both of something encountered and also of a being able to receive it.

Refusal to identify experience with but one of the factors that enters into its coming to exist does not preclude recognition of a clear asymmetry in the situation. What exists, what is there to be encountered, has its own mode of independence and insistence; the reality that confronts the experiencer maintains its own tenure, a tenure that does not depend on its being distinguished from the experiencer. In view of this fact, the being who has experience stands under a demand to *reflect* what is there to be encountered in a way that does full justice to the nature and being of the encountered material. This is the truth in the ancient philosophical doctrine of realism, and it explains why the discovery of what does exist is a difficult and arduous task. If reality encountered were no more than a tissue of the materials required for encountering, the discovery of and adjustment to what is there to be encountered would be a far easier enterprise than it is. The demand made by reality upon the experiencing being brings an asymmetry into the situation in which experience takes place. The experiencer must reflect what is there; what is encountered need reflect nothing.

On the other hand, the being capable of having experience also belongs to reality. This fact is frequently overlooked by those who preach an uncritical realism. It was also overlooked by those who regard the experiencer as a *tabula rasa* who merely reflects the scene "given" to him. The truth is that, if experience is a product of intersecting, structured elements, the being capable of experience will also have a structure and this structure will enter into the total process of experience. It is not a matter of allowing the one who experiences to make some "subjective" additions to be an otherwise totally independent reality; it is rather that experience is much more than a *reflection* or mirror image of what is encountered. The one who experiences *refracts* as well as *reflects*, and it is through such refraction that the material of encounter comes to be "taken" or interpreted in different contexts of meaning. The truth in the ancient idealist tradition in philosophy is expressed by saying that experience in the full and rich sense in which it comes to us is much more than the passive reception and consequent copying of what is given. The total nature of the being who experiences enters into the transaction, which means that the being is not simply a theoretical knower, but one who lives in and through experience, who puts questions both to the world and to himself, and who has an interest in experience as the source of life and understanding.

It is tempting to regard experience, insofar as it is the reflection of what exists, as the record of what is "really there," while supposing that the refractions are merely the result of subjective activity. This is an error. Just as there must be grounds in what is encountered for the faithful reflection of itself, so also must there be grounds for the refractions. These grounds will be different in the two cases; nevertheless, they will be grounds pointing to the natures of the two elements that intersect in the producing of experience.

The tendency to regard experience as a subjective affair, in contrast with so-called realistic approaches, finds its chief support in the belief that experience can be clearly defined in terms of some one characteristic derived from the psychological nature of the one who experiences. Thus experience came to be defined as the domain of sense or of feeling, in contrast both with systems of general or abstract ideas and with the physical world standing over against the human self. In the case of experience as interpreted through the eyes of the classical British empirical philosophers, the defining characteristic chosen was that of the simple, original unit of *sense* experience, taken as immediately present to the individual mind. But if experience is thus covered with a blanket characteristic such as sense and taken as something to be found only within the individual consciousness, the branding of experience as "subjective" is inevitable. Moreover, the restriction of experience to sense at once banishes from experience much that we actually encounter. It is a notorious fact, for example, that tendency or direction in a process cannot be fitted neatly into a pattern of experience defined by the standard senses. Colors, sounds, and odors were regarded by classical empiricists as clear and distinct apprehensions of sight, hearing, and the sense of smell, but the connections and transitions that tie these atomic ideas or feelings together did not seem to be the appropriate object of any sense whatever. Consequently, such connections were denied to be present in experience and, since they could not be ruled out entirely, had to be introduced as a constructive activity of the mind.

The difficulties raised by the restriction of experience to sense and its consequent location in the individual mind can be removed by refusing to identify experience with any single quality or characteristic, and especially by avoiding a characteristic that reduces experience to the sort of content that can be found only within the consciousness of an individual knower. Experience, understood as the funded result of many encounters with what is presented, is too rich and varied in content to be adequately described by any one predicate. There is no descriptive term comprehensive enough in meaning to express the entire content of experience as such. Experience is of events and things, of hopes and fears, of disappointments and expectations, of persons and places; in short, experience must be open to everything that is, and we are never justified in anticipating its content by assigning to it some specific and differential character purporting to express the sort of thing it *must* contain. A theory of experience does, of course, involve specifying a structure that is general; such a theory cannot be merely an exhaustive record of what is encountered. But the generality involved will take the form of an attempt to express the nature of experience as an activity and a way of approaching reality rather than a general description in terms of a single characteristic that is supposed to indicate the nature of the content experienced. What is encountered is matter for specific inquiry; experience as an activity connected with the life and thought of the one who experiences is matter for philosophical inquiry. And one function of an adequate philosophical theory is to challenge and criticize any attempt to short-circuit experience by confining it to some special content.

A further consequence of identifying experience with data of sense immediately present to the mind was the need to locate experience in the purely individual or isolated subject. Such data, it was argued, must be present to *someone* and, since such empiricism could make no provision for a super-individual consciousness, the singular individual subject was chosen as the locus of experience. The choice was fatal because it meant not only a failure to acknowledge the independent aspect of what is encountered or received by the one who has experience, but a radical subjectivizing of experience as well. For the experiencer is then alone and isolated; not only is experience taken as his own private stock of "ideas," but it becomes dependent on the individual sensible apparatus of the knower and is forced to appear as a mental or "psychological" content in contrast with the so-called external world. The charge that experience is subjective and insubstantial is an inevitable consequence of accepting such a theory. The question is whether the charge can be sustained if the theory on which it rests can be shown to be false.

There are at least two reasons for holding that the classical theory of experience must be rejected. First, there is no compelling need to suppose that *what* is experienced by an individual is identical with a set of data immediately apprehended and wholly confined to the mind of the experiencer; second, it is a fundamental error to omit the social or transindividual character of experience not only with respect to the relations between two distinct selves, but also with respect to the connections between the occasions of experience enjoyed by one and the same self enduring from moment to moment. The supposition that experience is made up of sensible data immediately apprehended by the mind as present to itself does not itself rest on any immediate apprehension that is incorrigible. The supposition is rather the result of a theory, although it has not always been so regarded. The need to identify the experiencer as a knower endowed with a capacity for certainty led to the supposition that if experience is restricted to the immediate content of the mind—to ideas, sense impressions, feelings—the experiencer can be certain about its content regardless of what may be the case with the object of experience in its own status beyond the self.

The important point is that the hypothetical character of this view be understood. No one can be said to be immediately aware and certain that what he claims to be immediately aware of is itself uniquely restricted to his own private consciousness. I may look in the direction of a lamp on a table and say, "whatever may be the truth about the so-called objective state of affairs falling beyond my consciousness, I am certain that I experience before my own mind a path of light that seems bright, surrounded by a darker region." Whether this statement is a reliable account of what actually happens or not, the fact remains that the claim that my experience of the lamp is identical with what is immediately present to one, single, private consciousness is *not* itself guaranteed by an immediate awareness or intuition; *it is instead a theory or inference.* When it was believed that, whereas I may be mistaken about lamps considered as physical objects, I cannot be mistaken about my "experience" of a lamp, the demand to have certainty was satisfied by confining our claims to the "experience" of the lamp, so that knowledge came to be not about the world but about our own ideas. There is no objection to holding such a view as a theory to be argued for (although even on this basis, it is inferior to other alternatives), but it is illegitimate to claim that this view of experience is guaranteed by an immediate insight. Let a man be aware immediately and certainly of anything you please, but there is no immediate insight enabling him to be certain that what he is thus immediately aware of is itself identical with his own private consciousness. That further claim is hypothetical and involves an inference. It is impossible to overestimate the importance of this point, for the entire tradition of interpreting experience in terms of a "mental" content immediately present to the experiencer and his individual mind has rested on the mistaken belief that this view of the situation is itself guaranteed by some sort of immediate insight. Exposure of the mistake involved shows the need for a reconsideration of the nature of experience; the idea that experience is no more than a private and subjective mental content is but one way of interpreting it. Such a view has no privileged status, and when it is forced to maintain itself in its true status as a theory it at once betrays its inadequacy.

Neglect of its social character has been a second major factor in establishing the view that experience is an insubstantial, subjective reflection of things. Experience is repeated encounter with what there is; it requires continuity and identity both in what is experienced and in the one who experiences. Experience is not possible as a collection of disconnected, momentary reports on the qualities that are disclosed through the senses; on the contrary, for reality to be given and received meaningfully it must be possible to identify items in such wise that we can make critical comparisons between different encounters of the same item. No item reveals itself fully and completely in an instant or in one encounter; repeated encounter is necessary, and this means that experience requires time and is involved in change. To represent development in the disclosure of a complex item of experience, repeated encounters must be connected with each other and thus come to have a cumulative effect or result. The social nature of experience enters at this point; every encounter exercises a critical function in relation to other encounters of the same item. The critical function of an encounter has long been recognized in the case of deliberate and controlled inquiry, where the experience of one inquirer is used to corroborate, invalidate, modify the experience of another. Here repeated encounter and the critical comparison of results depends explicitly on the co-operation of distinct selves. It is not, however, always understood that the social principle is operative within the continuing experience of a single self as well. The two situations are not, of course, comparable in every detail; there are features in the continuing relation of one self to itself at different times for which there will be no counterpart in the relations between two different selves. In both cases, however, a common pattern is exhibited, namely, the bringing of the isolated or purely individual encounter into relation with other encounters, thereby providing the means for critical sifting and the attainment of a result that is more reliable than any single encounter could be.

Experience is not something that can be confined to a single occasion or to an isolated individual. It is interesting to notice that appeals to experience always make reference to a cumulative product or to a deposit of insight or skill that has taken years to acquire. When we cite experience as a standard we never mean to point to a single occasion or to what is reported merely by a single individual. To say that a man "has experience" with riding horses or sailing invariably means that he has gained both knowledge and skill as a result of many encounters with horses or boats. A single or chance encounter clearly does not suffice. To speak of what "experience shows" when we are attempting to support a specific claim such as a prediction about the way in which a given social group will vote in an election, we always refer to the data of many occasions and the results of many experiences involving many people. The tendency of the older empiricism to think of experience in terms of singular, sharply demarcated occasions upon which an individual experiencer registers data received through his sense organs has been at the root of the widespread belief that experience is no more than a subjective product residing in the mind and is to be sharply contrasted with the so-called objective or external world. A reconsideration of what actually happens in the intersection between the one who experiences and the reality to be encountered will help to correct this mistake.

Experience must involve encounter in the sense that the one who has the experience must be co-existent with, and at the same time stand over against, what is there to be experienced. Coexistence distinguishes experience from "hearsay"—from reports about something which may be furnished for me by another without my being in the presence of the object about which the report is made. Encounter, on the other hand, though necessary, is not sufficient; the actualization of experience requires not only something to be encountered, but a sign-using animal capable of making discriminations and of expressing them in appropriate language. In actual experiencing, the two ingredients—the material of encounter and the one who encounters—go together. We do not start with a singular or isolated consciousness on one side and attempt to move out to a world of public fact. On the contrary, the self or person as a unique individual is discovered subsequently through reflection on actual experience of a public world. The experience of being a self distinct from a world of events and other selves is itself an event and one that is usually accompanied by a shock. The individual as a unique being with a measure of independence *vis à vis* other beings gains an awareness of itself at the point where it encounters its own power of discrimination, choice, preference, and judgment. At the moment when we discover that we have a *selective interest* in things, we become aware that we are individual, active beings and not merely passive "recorders" of given facts. Not everything is equally welcome to us; we seek to enjoy certain things and to avoid others. The self discovers itself as an agent of selection, of interest, and of critical judgment; the self becomes manifest through the experience of *responding* to what is encountered. The self as a reality with limits and boundaries, with a place and a date, comes before us when we encounter our own *interest* both in the world and in that limited being that responds to what is encountered. Without the shock of discovery that is the realization of interest—which means, in turn, preference and selection—the individual self would never come into view. Without interest, there would be only the unbroken flow of feeling and, while we might conceive of things being reflected from many points in the flow as the reflections of a mirror, there would be no awareness that these reflections were in any way connected with a self. That awareness comes only with the shock of interest and preference. If the self were no more than a recording apparatus copying the world, it is doubtful that it would ever become aware of its selfhood.

The problem of distinguishing between what is "really there" to be encountered and what belongs only to the nature of the self who encounters it is a problem that arises only after the self has been discovered. The distinction traditionally described as that between subject and object is not well formed within primitive or pre-theoretical encounter; that distinction is one that arises in the course of experience. The point is illustrated in the experience of every child; only gradually does he learn to set the world at a distance and distinguish himself from it. There is no warrant whatever for supposing that the individual self starts out *knowing* that all of its "experience" is private, personal, and confined wholly to its own consciousness, and that it then must find a way of surmounting that subjectivity in order to reach the "external world." That doctrine is in fact a theory and by no means a description of what actually happens in the development of experience. As a theory, moreover, it is prompted by the quest for certainty (if we cannot be certain of "objects" we can at least be certain of our ideas), and not by the aim of faithfully representing what is found to be the case. If we do not start out with the certainty that experience is something private and mental in character, and if, instead, we assume that in the course of experience the self is discovered, rather than being a fixed certainty at the outset, we have no need to hold to the view that experience as such has the status of the merely subjective or that it is confined to an individual consciousness.

There are indeed errors in experience and thus situations in which the one who experiences is mistaken. And errors do call for some distinction between the private and the public. There may be the conviction that one has encountered something which later fails to be supported by critical inquiry and reflection, and there may also be failure to notice what is there to be encountered so that we remain ignorant of its presence. But there is no need whatever to hold that these situations are correctly interpreted only in terms of purely private and subjective experience on one side and an "external" world on the other. A more adequate account of experience starts by allowing for the undeniable, realistic bias that controls ordinary experience and the sense that one encounters what is there to be encountered and not a set of private ideas, reports, or impressions. This realistic bias might continue undisturbed were it not for the discovery of the self and its characteristic activities, which in turn leads to the possibility of setting up an absolute distinction between purely private or mental content called "experience" and a world of things falling beyond the mind. The point is that with the discovery of the self comes the knowledge of the possibility of error and the need to distinguish between what is merely idiosyncratic and what is genuinely intersubjective or there to be encountered, by anyone, but there is no ground for supposing that we start with the certainty of a private mental content or experience on one side and an absolutely public or independent external world on the other. The logical outcome of such a supposition is the branding of experience as subjective or mental in character and the distortion of its actual nature.

The realistic bias that attaches to ordinary experience, the sense that in encountering the world we come up against something possessing its own insistence and independence, may seem less well-founded after the self has come clearly into view. For the self, with its interests and preferences, its purposes and plans, is bound to appear as a disturbing influence, a source of waywardness and error. And the temptation is very great to regard the self, taken as an individual, private scene of consciousness, as the perfect place in which to locate "experience" in contrast with the world of public objects. This private scene is then made into the repository of illusion and error so that the "real" external world can remain consistent and free of the subjective and conflicting reports about it that stem from supposedly private "experience." But there is no need to resolve problems that follow on the discovery of the self at the cost of transforming experience into a private, mental content. The errors and illusions that arise within experience can be detected and, where possible, eliminated only by further experience which is critical in character. The correction of experience, moreover, can be accomplished only if the doctrine of experience as private, mental content is given up, only if it becomes clear that experience does not exist in that form at the outset.

No amount of critical inquiry can transform private, mental content into a real world with independence of its own; reality is not the same as subjectivity standardized. If we begin in private, we end in private, and there is no escape from the circle. But the gnawing questions are: Do we begin in private? Must we acquiesce to the dogma which identifies experience only with the mental content of the private mind? The answer is no to both questions, because the dogma is not itself empirical, but rather a theory introduced in the first instance for the purpose of explaining error in the face of the belief that the real world is no more than the so-called primary qualities—extension, motion, shape, etc.—that are expressible in mathematical terms. The private-mind conception of experience is no deliverance of experience itself, but rather a device aimed at providing a handy receptacle in which to put impressions that seemed to contradict each other and in which to locate those features of the world that cannot be expressed in terms of mathematical physics.

When a theory leads to consequences that conflict with what we actually find to be the case, the proper procedure is not to invent a number of *ad hoc* hypotheses in order to tame the theory, but to call the theory into question by returning to the starting point. We are thus led back to primary experience and to the discovery that the initial error lay in the belief that experience is the same as a private, mental content that stands in total contrast to a public or so-called external world. Experience at every stage of its development from the simplest to the most complex retains its basic nature as *encounter;* and encounter always involves the one who experiences and the what of experience. Experience is at the very least a dyadic affair and it is even possible that it is irreducibly triadic in character, but it is certainly not monadic in the sense of being bare, sensible content. Unless experience is understood as relation to a world encountered beyond the self at the outset, there is no way out of the closed circle of mental life to a reality beyond. And if we are told that this is precisely our predicament, that we can never reach the external world because we are confined to our own mental life, we must ask how it is that we are supposed to know that our starting point is private, mental content. If there is no need to start with the assumption—and it must always be an assumption because we are never *immediately certain* that what we have "before us" or are "aware of" is only a private, mental content—that experience is a mere tissue of subjectivity, then there is no need to break out of the circle of subjectivity by desperate logical moves and epistemological theories. For too long the burden of proof has been misplaced. For too long it has been supposed that experience is a mental affair and that we begin our relations with the world confined to an "inside" view so that the problem is that of finding ways to move to the world "outside." But if the dogma about experience as private, mental content is challenged as a nonempirical and erroneous view of experience, the problem is transformed. Breaking "out" of subjectivity is not the problem because we were never confined to the "inside" in the first place. Experience may mislead us and it may be mistaken, but not because it is merely subjective ideas and feelings; experience could not lead to real error if it were not an actual encounter with and participation in a real world that transcends human consciousness in every direction.

A further consequence of the classical theory of experience is found in loss of the dimensions of meaning or contexts in which the materials of experience are taken. The idea of experience as a succession of data given to and received by an individual mind served to identify the self largely as a theoretical knower of the world and, in turn, reduced the world to the status of a collection of phenomena waiting to be known and explained. Experience was considered solely in terms of content—qualities and their conjunctions as objects—and less attention was paid to the dimensions of experience, the different contexts of meaning within which the items of experience can be said to figure. Or if these dimensions were taken into account, they were put down to the interpreting mind and not seen as dimensions *of* experience. The result was an impoverishment of experience. But experience is not the same as the passive reception of colors and sounds identified and named; experience involves as well frameworks of meaning within which what we encounter is interpreted and evaluated. These frameworks coincide with the capacity of things to enter into various relations both with each other and with the one who experiences. One and the same object, for example, may figure in many different dimensions of experience, depending on its nature and the purposes of the experiencing self. The familiar dimensions or "worlds" of meaning designated by the terms "morality," "art," "economics," "history," "religion," and others represent so many standpoints from which the things of the world can be taken and understood. To cite a simple instance, a table is experienced not merely as a collection of data that fall together in a space, but as an item that has value in exchange, as a piece of craftsmanship that delights us because of the shape or form into which it has been fashioned, as an object of historical interest because it provides us with knowledge about men who lived in the past and their ways, as a symbol pointing to the possibilities inherent in original material believed to have been created by God. Not every common object, to be sure, will figure in every possible dimension of experience, but every such object *could* so figure, depending upon the particular circumstances.

Though the different dimensions of experience are familiar enough in daily life, their precise nature and connection with experience has not always been understood. The dimensions of experience are a result of two factors: first, the multiple character of the items of experience and their capacities to enter into different kinds of relations with other items, and second, the purposes of the self in confronting the world and in seeking to find self-realization. Neither factor should be given priority over the other; both belong together in actual experience. It is an error to suppose that the dimensions of experience represent nothing more than human ways of taking things so that, for example, the temporal and historical character of what is encountered reduces to man's interest in himself and his past. Conversely, it is equally mistaken to suppose that there is an objective domain of "neutral fact" devoid of all direction and purpose in itself and waiting to be endowed with a meaning stemming from the human mind. A more adequate account of the dimensions of experience will hark back to the basic character of experience as encounter of the intersection between what exists and the experiencing self. The ensuing product of encounter is a unique synthesis, derived from the two intersecting terms. On the one hand, the reality encountered has capacities for sustaining the many relations that constitute the different dimensions; the table *has* a value in exchange, it *has* an aesthetic surface, it *is* a sign of the past.

On the other hand, the experiencing self has many purposes in confronting the world, and some significant aspect of its own life is expressed through each of the dimensions; the self enjoys the world of art, it seeks for its ultimate destiny in the world of religion, it pursues the good life and judges its own performance in the world of morality. There is a constant correlation between the two elements that constitute experience; the items encountered have capacities for entering into the dimensions of experience and the self expresses its own purposes in acknowledging these capacities. The aesthetic dimension of experience, for example, is possible because both natural objects and the materials from which works of art are fashioned have capacities for embodying aesthetic form; the self, on the other hand, has a purpose and interest in such form so that in recognizing it and in helping to create new forms the self enhances its own realization.

The dimensions of experience belong to experience itself. They represent a co-operation of factors and best illustrate the interpenetration of the nature of what is encountered and the purposes of the one who encounters. Failure to acknowledge the existence of these dimensions in experience has been largely responsible for the wide-spread view that experience is no more than a domain of "fact" without further significance in itself. If this is so, it follows that these dimensions can be no more than subjective additions, merely human ways of looking at things, that come after the fact, so to speak, and have no foundations in reality encountered. But such a view is itself at variance with what we find to be the case with regard to empirical science. The concept of "fact" in the sense of a sharply delineated content describable in terms of universally applicable categories is one that has been constructed for the special purposes of theoretical science. As an abstraction, this concept is well founded and serves admirably the purposes for which it was intended. But it is absolutely illegitimate to suppose that such "fact" has superior status as being *the* fundamental and final expression of the nature of reality. For the data that are taken to be the primary facts in any highly precise science are conditioned by the further fact that they have been abstracted for a special purpose—that of theoretical, causal explanation—and are described in terms of the most abstract categories—number, position, shape, etc. That such abstractions can be well founded is not denied; what is denied is that the representation of what is encountered in the special terms of theoretical science results in a "neutral" disclosure of reality itself in a privileged form. The enterprise of theoretical science itself forms one of the dimensions of experience and only so much of reality is disclosed through it as is consistent with the general purposes guiding and controlling the theoretical investigation of things. Failure to recognize the limiting conditions that define the dimension of experience constituting science has led to the belief that the highly abstract descriptions offered by theoretical science represent *the* basic nature of things and that consequently all the other dimensions in which things can be taken and understood are no more than subjective additions to the neutral facts. The first step toward the correction of the oversight is taken when we have a proper understanding of the place of science as only one among the many dimensions of experience. There are other dimensions based on other purposes and each has its own part to play in the disclosure of reality.

It is necessary to call attention to the limiting or boundary conditions of science in order to make it possible to escape from a twofold tyranny over the other dimensions of experience exercised in the name of science (though not always with the approval of those who are really scientists). First is the supposition just indicated, according to which abstract, theoretical knowledge represents the disclosure of reality in a privileged form. Second is the demand that all the dimensions of experience other than that of theoretical science stand under obligation to produce credentials in accordance with the same conditions that govern the pursuit of scientific knowledge. Such a demand stands in open contradiction to the fact that there are many different purposes behind the various dimensions of experience and, while it is essential to every dimension to represent reality as it is actually encountered, it is by no means obvious that this result can be achieved in only one way. The interpretations of human life and the world that are to be found in the dimensions of religion or morality, for example, are not of the same logical type as the account of reality that is given in any of the natural sciences. Reality as apprehended through those sciences must, of course, be taken into account; a rational religion or morality must remain responsive to what is disclosed about things, including themselves, from the scientific dimension. But what must be exposed as no more than an assumption, though natural enough in view of the dazzling success and prestige of natural science, is the claim that the conditions governing the acquisition of theoretical knowledge are appropriate for every dimension of experience.

The relative autonomy of the various dimensions requires, *per contra*, that appropriate critical principles be devised for each one: two rival theories or interpretations in physics, for example, are related to each other in a way vastly different from the way in which the Christian doctrine of creation is related to the Buddhist doctrine of eternality that makes creation unnecessary. In view of examples of this sort, it is clear that no single set of conditions governing any one dimension of experience can be made universal and legislative for all dimensions. Unless this restriction is acknowledged, the inevitable consequence is the reduction of experience to but one of its dimensions, and, in the current situation, this is likely to be the dimension of theoretical science.

If experience has often been condemned as insubstantial and unreliable because of its supposed subjectivity, it has suffered no less at the hands of those who insist upon approaching experience solely through the medium of expression. The "linguistic turn," as it may be called, has come to dominate modern thought; the approach to philosophical problems through the analysis of language represents the final step in the development of critical philosophy in which the attempt is made to deal with these problems solely in terms of the *general conditions* for experience, for thought, or for the language in which the result is to be expressed. Experience demands expression of some kind, and there is no denying that the form of the expression is neither accidental in character nor wholly external to what is expressed. Even the experience of identity with God or the ultimate reality characteristic of mysticism is often given symbolic expression as in such expressions as the "sacred silence" or the "flight of the alone to the alone." But from the proposition that experience demands expression in language or some symbolic medium—which is true—it does not follow that everything encountered actually does find expression or that all of what does find expression has been adequately expressed. Moreover, if experience is not an instantaneous affair but a process requiring time, it follows that there is a "move" from encounter to expression. Two consequences follow: first, every form of expression (term, symbol, etc.) that has an established use will reflect what has *already been encountered*, and second, the move to expression is liable to error because it means passing from what is *encountered* to *what* is encountered, from the reality presented to its naming and description. No such move is immediately guaranteed; whether we have correctly expressed what is there can be ascertained only by subsequent encounters, and not merely by the further analysis of expressions and their meaning. Any approach that is confined exclusively to the analysis of expressions already established in use is dealing, *ipso facto*, with reports, descriptions, and interpretations of what has already figured in some encounter. If we confine discussion to the analysis of these expressions, we are in danger of losing what can be disclosed only in fresh encounters with the referents of these expressions. For, as much analysis shows, the linguistic philosopher may be tempted to abandon the need for returning to encounter, preferring instead to remain within the linguistic circle marked out by the expressions he has selected, manipulating them according to logical rules.

There is no need to deny the positive contribution that can be made to the apprehension and understanding of experience by the linguistic approach, but there are at least three difficulties posed that reveal its limitations as *the* philosophical method. First, there is the restriction of experience that follows from treating it entirely in terms of *general* conditions or factors that are supposed to hold for "all possible experience" but which in fact are never sufficient for totally determining any singular, actual experience. As Kant's critical philosophy shows, when it comes to the anticipation of experience it is not possible to do more than anticipate its general shape; actual experience always transcends every such anticipation, even when our grasp of the conditions of possible experience is an adequate one. In other words, it is not necessary to deny validity to the general conditions of experience (or expression) in order to point out that, however accurately we have apprehended these conditions, they are insufficient of themselves to determine absolutely any singular experience. The need for encounter cannot be eliminated.

The second difficulty concerns the restrictive function exercised over experience by the normative role assigned to language. In approaching experience solely through the medium of its expression it is possible that some one function of language or some set of rules for governing the use of language will be set up as *the* model for language in all of its functions and forms. When this happens experience is subjected to great strain and much that is actually encountered tends to be ignored while certain of the dimensions of experience are ruled out as "noncognitive" or merely the expression of emotion. The development of positivism nicely illustrates the consequences of supposing that the "original" single function of language is to "convey information" so that only the language of natural science is admitted as valid (plus, of course, the language required for logical apparatus, transformation rules, etc.) And the further history of positivism shows that even the language of science could not meet the original positivist requirements in terms of which it was to be decided whether a given expression "conveys information" or not. The resolution of that particular problem, however, is not as important as the fact that singling out the one function of language as that of conveying information had the effect of eliminating the religious, metaphysical, moral, and aesthetic dimensions of experience from the domain of cognitive import.

The choice of the language of formal logic as the model language for the expression of experience places the greatest possible strain on experience and has the effect of filtering out of our elemental encounter with the world all but those aspects that can be universalized and given the most precise expression. Dissatisfaction with the severe restrictions on what could be said—restrictions imposed by the demand that the language of logic * should be the primary form of expression—produced a reaction that has resulted in the acknowledgment of many languages and uses of language, each with some measure of autonomy. The concern for the language of logic gave way to the search for the logic of this or that language in actual use. Admission of a multitude of languages leaves the door open for the possibility of expressing the full range of experience in its many dimensions. Although the fact is not always noticed, the appeal to so-called "ordinary language"—not only in the sense of the language used to express "common sense" understanding of things, but also to express our ordinary or customary experience—as the measure for every use of language is no less objectionable than the singling out of the language of logic as the basic norm. It happens that ordinary language is more concrete, and it enshrines in itself more of what is actually encountered than logical language can express, but the appeal to ordinary language can be equally reductive as is shown by its use in the dissolution of metaphysical thought. There is no reason why what people ordinarily say should exercise control over the description and interpretation of experience. Language is always "in gear" when it is being used to express what is encountered in experience and interpreted through its dimensions. The claim that language is "idling" when it is used to express what, for example, theologians and speculative philosophers want to say, is a case of special pleading that can never be justified except in a dogmatic way.

The third difficulty raised by the approach to experience through the medium of expression concerns the indirectness involved and the consequent identification of philosophical interpretation with critical or second order questions. Concentration

* By the phrase "language of logic" I mean such expressions, both words and symbols, as are used for logical constants, quantifiers, etc., by contemporary logicians. For example, Russell's attempt to construe *existence* as meaning that a certain propositional function is sometimes true would be a case of what I mean by the casting of a philosophical doctrine into the "language of logic."

on what is said or on well-formed expressions presumed to be given either in ordinary discourse or in the special language of some special inquiry may well lead to the neglect of actual experience as it happens. Language, like the "ideas" of the classical empiricists or the "sense data" of more recent empiricism, in time assumes the form of a barrier standing between the experiencing self and what is there to be encountered. Thinking becomes abstract in the special sense that the primary subject matter does not come directly into view; for example, one thinks not about history as a dynamic continuum of *events*, but rather about historical writing or language, and tries to approach the subject by considering the forms of expression and the relations between them. More often than not, starting with language means concentrating on the topic in question solely in terms of theoretical knowledge. From considering the language of history one tends to pass on to the question of historical knowledge and to the justification of statements or assertions, so that many aspects of the historical dimension of experience are lost. Statements, of course, must be made before we have history expressed in record, but this necessity does not alter the fact that actual history is more than a record. The same holds true for other dimensions of experience; persons and places, things and events, institutions and traditions, all gradually fall from sight when experience is subordinated to expression. But experience never fails to transcend expression, which is why it is always necessary to return to actual encounter in order to criticize our verbal expressions.

II
The Religious Dimension of Experience and the Idea of God

Interpreting religion as a dimension of experience is not the same as interpreting God and religion by means of the concept of "religious experience." That concept was introduced into the discussion largely by the efforts of William James and others to give an empirical account of the nature of religion, and it came to mean—as it did in part for James—the identification of religion with certain specific kinds of feeling. The feelings singled out for special attention were, for the most part, associated with the sense of a "Presence" not human or finite in character, the sense of peace, joy, and being "saved," the sense of the holy or that which commands worship and respect. Sometimes, but not always, the crucial moments of religious experience were identified with mystical phenomena or with some form of immediate awareness vividly felt by an individual person. Insofar as religion must involve the engagement of the individual self, intensely personal experiences will never be irrelevant to an understanding of its nature. But certain problems are raised by the appeal to "religious experience" that need to be brought forth and considered in a critical light. For it is likely that the proper contribution of experience to an understanding of God and the religious life may be obscured by the supposition that this contribution must be found only in the special doctrine of "religious experience."

Three difficulties will prevent the circumspect from settling the problem of the experiential foundation of religion by appealing to religious experience as it came to be understood after James and in the writings of "empirical" theologians. The first and most formidable obstacle is that the citing of some special states of the total self as the original data for religion and as the "facts" that need to be interpreted philosophically and theologically gives credence to the supposition than an experiential approach means no more than an attempt to reduce God to a tissue of human experience and to constitute religion in a way that makes it unnecessary to appeal to a disclosure from beyond man's consciousness. A second difficulty is found in the legitimate criticisms that have been launched against the attempt to claim a parallelism between religion and scientific inquiry in that both are said to begin with facts and to base their doctrines on these facts. More than one critic has raised a question about the justification by which one can claim to have shown the "existence" of God, for example, by appeal to the "facts" of religious experience. The third difficulty with the approach through religious experience is that it tends to perpetuate the view of experience as a set of singular, hard data, present to the mind of the individual self. If this conception of the general nature of experience is inadequate, it is no less inadequate for representing the experiential foundation of religion.

Religion, as we shall have to make clear, is a relation that holds in living experience between an individual person and the object of worship eliciting from us reverence and love. Religion itself is not the object of worship, although it has frequently happened that man has made the visible religious institution the center of his concern. This displacement or disorientation is most likely to occur in skeptical periods of history when belief in the reality of God declines and the attempt is made to preserve "religion" without God. But such an attempt must fail because religion demands an object of worship other than and beyond the self; moreover, if idolatry is to be avoided, the object of worship cannot be any finite or conditioned object whatever. The religious relationship demands an absolute allegiance which distinguishes it from all limited loyalties having finite objects and causes as their aim. The religious object,* therefore, cannot be identical with feelings or states of the finite self even if such feelings and states do indeed play a part in the religious life. The experience of the individual—his faith, his hopes, his ideals, his love—belongs to religion, but such experience does not exhaust religion nor does the inner life of the self constitute the religious object. Much confusion has arisen on this point. Without some form of presence in personal experience, God can have no meaning for an individual, but from this fact it does not follow that God or the religious object is *identical* with any finite experience. The attempt to find the meaning of basic religious concepts such as faith, love, guilt, atonement, etc., in the actual experience of the individual must not be understood in a reductive sense as an attempt to equate the religious object with finite experiences or states of the experiencing subject. We begin in our understanding of every phenomenon with what is most accessible to us. Since man is the religious animal, the one in whom the religious concern becomes explicit, we begin naturally enough with man and his experience. But from the fact that some reality enters into experience, it does not follow that it is thereby transformed into a merely "psychological" reality. From a logical point of view there is no more reason for supposing that ex-

* By the term "religious object" is meant the reality to which an unconditional love or absolute devotion is directed. The term is meant to stand for a general category in view of the fact that the philosophy of religion must treat religion in generic terms. Its categories must not be confined to any one religious tradition. We cannot, therefore, use the term "God" instead of "religious object" because "God" is the name for that reality within the Judeo-Christian tradition. The difficulty remains even if we hold that there is a concept of God and that the term is not only a name. The important point is that it is necessary to have an expression such as "religious object" (awkward though it is) in order to describe whatever it is which functions in any tradition as the reality to which supreme devotion is directed.

periences in which God is believed to be present *ipso facto* transform God into a pyschological reality than there is for believing that our experience of, for example, an ordinary table thereby transforms it into a psychological reality. We may admit that the appeal to religious experience understood as a tissue of interior states of the soul easily gives rise to the view that the religious object is being reduced to something merely human. But the confusion is not necessary. If experience is understood as encounter, there is no difficulty whatever in supposing that a reality can be ingredient in experience while also transcending—in the sense of not being identical with—that experience.

In the religious situation, encounter leads at once to the idea of a divine disclosure, or, in religious language, revelation. It is sometimes thought that approaching religion through experience means a denial of what has been understood in the Christian tradition as revelation. On the contrary, experience understood as encounter is always disclosure of reality transcending the one who experiences. Not every interpretation of revelation will be acceptable from a critical point of view; a defensible account of divine disclosure remains as a task to be accomplished. But it is important to notice that there is no necessary incompatability between experience and revelation. Two considerations are of prime importance: that a philosophical account of religion in experiential terms does not aim at constituting or "constructing" either God or the religious relationship; and that experience properly understood requires that some place be made for encounter, for the experiencing self to meet what is other than itself, whatever that "other" may turn out to mean. A grasp of these two considerations and their implications will show why it is a mistake to criticize the experiential approach for failing to allow for divine disclosure.

With regard to the first point, understanding the religious relationship and the meaning of the religious object in terms of human experience does not imply reducing either to a "merely human" level. Religion in both individual and institutional form is something that we encounter as a reality to be understood. As such, religion does not need to be "constructed" by the philosopher. What the philosopher has to say about religion may well have its influence on the development of theology and religious belief, but it is neither the aim nor the task of the philosopher to create religion and still less is it his business to "construct" God out of the supposed data of religious experience. If there are certain types of experience in which God may be said to be ingredient, that will be a matter for interpretation and critical argument, but such interpretation is not to be construed as an attempt to reduce God to either purely immanent experience or to states of consciousness. The realities we encounter and the dimensions of experience in and through which they are interpreted are not the creations of the philosophical intelligence. In this sense the philosopher is not called upon to produce, but rather to understand, what experience affords. Philosophical interpretation does mean transformation of what is interpreted, and therefore we cannot say that the philosopher merely "analyzes" or clears up a content given to him. But the transformation does not *constitute* what he is interpreting. This point holds no less for religion than for morality, art, and science. It is not that the philosopher is forced to accept everything at face value; it is rather that he is forced to accept what he finds. If the task is to discover the nature of religion, religion must be taken in the first instance as a fact, and no interpretation, whether in terms of experience or not, will be adequate if it concludes by saying that there was no reality to be interpreted in the first place.

If this is so, there will be no necessity for supposing that interpreting religion and the religious object in terms of experience means a denial of revelation and the possibility of divine disclosure. For the idea of a divine disclosure belongs essentially to religion as something that is constituted apart from the interpreting mind. Revelation is one of the factors that an empirically oriented philosopher will have to take into account, and if he finds it a problem or an idea that needs careful scrutiny, that will not change the fact that it must be reckoned with. If, on the other hand, the philosopher supposes that giving a philosophical account of religion means providing a "rational" interpretation which excludes at the outset the possibility of divine disclosure in any sense, then we must answer that he is prejudging the case and, even more, that he is not paying attention to actual religion as we find it but is instead giving his own view of what religion is, or what it ought to be, or even further, what it *would* be if it were truly "rational." An experiential approach rules out such a prejudgment and, far from precluding the possibility of revelation, actually demands that it be considered if we are to reflect the facts as we find them. The philosopher is to interpret religion, not create it.

With regard to the charge that approaching religion through religious experience means reducing God to human experience, it is necessary only to repeat what has been said about the need for encounter. Concentration upon religious experience as something confined to the individual consciousness has been responsible for the widespread belief that if one begins with experience, it will be impossible to allow for the disclosure of God from beyond the limits of the self. But if experience always means encounter of some sort, then the possibility of revelation or divine disclosure remains open and constitutes a matter for further discussion. This is all that is required for an experiential approach —namely, that it not entail the impossibility of revelation at the outset.

The second major difficulty which has been associated with the notion of religious experience touches on the complex question of the divine existence. It has been argued, notably by Dewey and others, that it is illegitimate to cite religious experience as the data that "prove" the existence of God as if the case were the same as citing sensory data in support of the claim that some particular sensible thing exists. Since God is not a sense object, the objection may be admitted and even insisted upon; the occurrence of certain experiences in the life of a person do not stand to God as the appearances of a sensible object stand to the object itself. A pure empiricism of immediacy such as can be found in mysticism, where God is disclosed without a medium, as it were, would seem to demand that the reality or existence of God be given along with the immediate experience itself. If, however, we deny that there can be an absolutely immediate experience that is also meaningful, it follows that any supposed experience of God would have to be mediated in some way. Expressed in different language, every alleged experience of God would also be experience of something else at the same time. If this is so, no singular experience would stand in analogy with a sensible experience of an object as evidence that God exists. From this, however, it does not follow that a divine reality may not be ingredient in human experience in the sense that there are mediating elements in existence that will disclose the presence of God.

The mistake embodied in the idea of religious experience as set forth by James and the so-called empirical theology consists in the acceptance of an absolute distinction between immediacy and mediation, or between immediate experience and inference. On the one hand, it was felt that religion is too intimate an affair to be a matter of rationalistic doctrines supported by a God whose reality is merely inferred without being experienced. On the other, it was believed that the only alternative to the rationalist approach is to be found in immediate data of experience that would represent, in James's expression, the "cash value" of the divine reality. Perhaps there is a third possibility that avoids the difficulties of both points of view. For if an experiential approach does not mean that God must be a matter of absolutely immediate experience, some third alternative in the form of *interpreted experience* may provide the answer. There must be a way beyond and between absolute immediacy and inference. Absolute immediacy can never deliver what it promises because some form of mediation—concepts, language, symbols—always intervenes and makes it impossible to pass from the experience to the reality of God; inference does not suffice because it always takes the form of necessity, which means not that God is experienced, but that something else is experienced and that therefore God "must" be real. The deficiencies of the two approaches point the way to a third approach, that of mediated or interpreted experience in which both experience and interpretation are interwoven. In this approach all relevant features of the situation are taken into account. The peculiar character of the reality of God is acknowledged together with the corresponding need for a medium of disclosure, and the medium is shown to be related in an intimate way to the reality it discloses. Both experience and mediation are thus allowed for; it is possible to avoid the difficulties that attach to an experience that cannot legitimately point beyond itself and an inference which leaves the self without experience *of* the reality of God but only of something else.

The third problem connected with the original idea of religious experience, the idea of experience as hard data present in the individual mind, has been sufficiently treated in other connections. The idea was too obviously patterned after the classical conception of experience, with its clear-cut data of sense and its psychological connotations, to be satisfactory as a theory of experiential foundations in religion. If the classical conception fails as a theory of the general nature of experience, it also fails as an account of the place of experience in religion. The religious life cannot be equated with a series of states of the self each of which is regarded as a special influx of the reality of God. This crude conception brings with it the vision of a theoretical spectator who "sees" apparitions or "senses" the presence of strange forces, as if the entire business of religion were a topic for theoretical explanation. Just as the classical conception of experience was developed largely for the purposes of explaining science and a strictly cognitive approach to the world, the interpretation of religion in terms of religious experience suggests that religion is primarily a matter of proposing and testing hypotheses. For the religious person, however, the religious life has its own depth and significance; God endows the whole of life with a dominant purpose within which a person lives and moves. Such testing of faith as does take place cannot be accomplished wholly from outside by a spectator who is "neutral" and without personal involvement. And in any case the religious stance is not that of science and the theoretical standpoint. There is a *life* of religion; there is no life of science in the same sense. The theoretical standpoint is a limited one and does not satisfy the self as a whole, although this standpoint as expressed in the pursuit of scientific knowledge is often made to serve as if it were a form of total life. We sometimes speak of the life of a "man of science" as if this could be a life style sufficient unto itself. But even if such a life of science were viable, it would take us beyond science, for when we speak of the pursuit of scientific knowledge as a way of life, we thereby endow science with a final purpose, that is, we declare that the pursuit of theoretical knowledge is an end in itself. But even then it does not satisfy, because a man is not identical with a theoretical knower. The approach to religion through the idea of religious experience was associated with the idea of a spectator who observes the phenomena without participating in them. Insofar as we approach religion in such a way, we fail to understand its nature.

Some have taken note of the difficulties connected with the doctrine of religious experience, but instead of searching for other ways of expressing the empirical foundations of religion, they have abandoned experience altogether, turning instead to dogmatic theology, to liturgy, to language, to history. This is an error. Whatever importance attaches to these other factors in religion, it cannot long survive without empirical roots. It is a mistaken course, both philosophically and religiously, to abandon experience to a narrow empiricist understanding of its nature while searching elsewhere for other foundations for religion that must turn out in the end to be less substantial and less concrete.

If a narrow conception of experience excludes an understanding of religion in experiential terms, then so much the worse for that conception. Experience itself demands that we abandon such conceptions, if need be, in order to do justice to the facts.

The proper interpretation of religion in terms of human experience coincides with the correct description, *not* of religious experience, but of the *religious dimension of experience.* Among the many dimensions or "worlds" of meaning in which experience is taken and through which it is understood, stands the religious dimension, the dimension in which all is understood from the perspective of the worshipful being. This dimension marks man as the religious animal in the sense that he is the one being in whom the question of the purpose of existence as such becomes explicit both as a *question* and as a supreme *interest.* All finite and limited realities have their being hedged in by limitations, by a finite span of life, by conflict and struggle with other beings. To this law man is no exception. He differs from all other finite beings, however, in his ability to envisage a whole of existence—in part through conception and in part through imagination—and to ask for a final purpose for that whole. Man is the one being in finite existence who asks about the quality of existence as such. The asking, moreover, is no purely theoretical matter such as is the case with questions that may or may not be answered in a man's lifetime. The question about the final purpose of the whole is at the same time a question to which every man *needs* some sort of answer as a basis for his *present* existence.

Understanding the religious dimension solely in terms of an interest that human beings display and a question about the purpose of existence is inadequate unless it is also shown how this question and interest are related to the religious question of God. For, as has not always been understood, the *religious* question about God is not one more theoretical question concerning what things are in existence. It is not a question of precisely the same sort as that of asking whether universals exist, or whether there exist living beings on other planets. The reason for the difference is that in asking about the reality of God we are at the same time asking about the purpose of our own existence; the one who asks the question is asking about a reality that concerns his own existence as well as the divine existence. The reality of God in the religious sense is also an answer to the question, is there a purpose for existence as a whole? The religious significance of the question of God has often been lost in the course of dealing with the traditional arguments for God's existence. The result has been that such discussions are often no more than a field for the display of logical ingenuity in which the term "God" means nothing more than a concept, or at most another thing that may or may not be real. The point is of the utmost importance, for it is essential to an experiential approach that the question of the purpose of existence as such—the question that identifies man as the religious animal—be understood, at the same time, as the question of God. Unless this connection is grasped, the experiential approach collapses into a psychological or phenomenological study of man and the introduction of God becomes superfluous. The approach through experience is most vulnerable at this point; we must not stop by noting the fact that human beings raise the question of the purpose of existence and that they have a supreme interest in the answer; we must go on to show that the question and interest point to God as the answer. Theological critics are correct in their objections to the experiential approach only to the extent to which reference to God is omitted. But the omission of this crucial reference is by no means necessary to an experiential approach. The fact is that we are enabled to identify the religious dimension of experience in the first instance because we see that in participating in that dimension man is asking for God as the only possible answer to his question.

The connection between the religious dimension of experience and the idea of God can be made explicit by analyzing that dimension itself and by showing how the experience of the holy forms the experiential content of God disclosed in human experience. The first task is best accomplished by directing attention to the basic distinction between the holy and the profane. For it is involvement with the holy, both in distinction from and in relation to the profane, that characterizes the religious dimension in its essential nature. The first point to notice is that the terms "holy" and "profane," like their near-synonyms "sacred" and "secular," have taken on moral (if not moralistic) connotations that are likely to be confusing. "Secular" is used with a pejorative connotation by some theologians in describing contemporary society, and to call something "sacred" frequently means no more than that it is highly prized in human terms and thus not to be treated indifferently or violated. The terms "holy" and "profane" are more suitable because they have not become as completely identified with these valuational connotations as their near-synonyms.

The holy and the profane stand in polar relation to each other; in one sense they are antithetical because what is holy stands over against the profane and cannot be dissolved into it, and yet the two must not be interpreted so that all relations between them are severed. It belongs to the nature of the holy to make its appearance in and through the profane, and it belongs to the nature of the profane to be sustained and illuminated by the holy.

The key to understanding the holy in experience is to be found in the contrast between the ordinary activities of human life—waking, nourishing ourselves, working, replenishing our energy through taking rest and recreation—and those special times or junctures in life that are set apart from the ordinary course of events and "celebrated" as having some peculiar meaning and seriousness about them. These special times, sometimes called the "crises" or turning points in life, are regarded in all cultures as extraordinary times that are somehow set apart from the rest of life. The time of being born, the time of attaining puberty or entering into adult life, the time of initiation into the social community or of confirmation (baptism, etc.) into the religious community, the time of choosing a vocation, the time of marriage, the time of giving birth, the time of death; these are the special times at which the holy becomes manifest. Identifying these events in human life as turning points endowed with peculiar significance because they involve the holy is a far easier task than expressing precisely what it is about them that causes us to set them apart and to celebrate them. The idea of *celebration* furnishes an initial key, as does also the fact that times for celebration are marked off as "holidays," in religious language, "holy days."

Celebration here does not mean primarily making merry or escaping from the daily round through enjoyment, although festive eating and drinking are generally associated with the celebration of the extraordinary events in a person's life. Celebration means being awed, fascinated, and even overpowered by the special events as a result of acknowledging that they are times when a sense of the mystery of all being and of one's own being is forced upon us. There is the sense that at these times we are in the presence of the supremely powerful, what has control over our destiny, what is the supremely important reality that is alone worthy of worship. The utter fascination of such occasions gives rise to celebration, a form of ritual intended to preserve or perpetuate the record of the event and its power. The effort at preservation within the act of celebration has two aspects: first, there is the actual *marking off* of the event as something more than an event beside others and its removal from the cycle of anonymous events of the daily round; second, there is the aim of *retaining* the event in memory, of keeping it from passing away by associating with it other experiences that intensify its quality. Except for marriage and childbirth, the distinguishing feature of each of the crucial junctures of life is that they cannot be repeated; there is a "once-for-all" character about them that stands in marked contrast to the ordinary events of life taking place again and again.

The existence of crucial events in the cycle of human life has been acknowledged in all cultures, and they have always been set apart and celebrated because of their peculiar significance. What remains to be made clear is precisely why these events should be of special importance for understanding the holy in human experience. The answer is twofold: in the first place, these events have been called, aptly enough, "crises" in human life because they are times when the purpose of life as such comes into question and when we have the sense that life is being judged, not in its details, but as a whole; in the second, the crisis times fill us with a sense of the finitude and frailty of man, of our creatureliness, of our dependence upon resources beyond our own, and of our need to find a supremely worshipful reality to whom we can devote ourselves without reserve. In both cases it is the source and quality of our being that is forced into the foreground of our consciousness; the crisis times are filled with power because for the time being they set at nought all preliminary concerns and direct our thoughts away from the banality of ordinary life to dwell, with awe and proper seriousness, upon the mystery of life itself. It is of the utmost importance to notice that in the records of many primitive religions the times of crisis are regarded as "dangerous" times, because it is at such times that the natural order comes in contact with or is touched by the unseen world and its power. Apart from the crudity and superstition often associated with such beliefs, there remains an important truth in these interpretations. It is as if the times of crisis were so many openings into the depth of life, into its ground, its purpose, its finite character. Ordinary life, "profane" existence, just because it is subjected to habit and routine, remains on the surface and covers the depth. A life that exists only on the surface gradually loses the capacity to acknowledge or to respond in awe to life in its depth and must be shocked into a realization of the holy on the special occasions when the holy ground of life is celebrated. A completely profane existence is one in which the ordinary events of life, no matter how bizarre, exciting, cruel, tragic they may be in themselves, exclude all sense of awe and mystery, so that even the crisis times themselves become ordinary times, occasions for merriment or "relaxation," and the depth aspect of life no longer has any meaning. Whether it is possible to achieve a complete profanization of life remains a question, but for many people the times of crisis have lost their power and no longer elicit an acknowledgment of the holy ground of all life.

Profane existence means an existence which is open, manifest, transparent, obvious, taken for granted, ordinary, and thus lacking all mystery and power. Ordinary occasions are precisely those that do not involve matters of "life and death" so that they fail to quicken in us an attitude of contemplation over the mystery of life itself and its purpose. It is not that profane life is valueless or that it should be degraded or despised; on the contrary, profane existence forms by far the largest part of our life, but in contrast with the crucial times, the daily round of events is ordinary enough and gives no occasion for wonder or special concern. In the ordinary events there is no question of a judgment on life as a whole. We do not celebrate the ordinary events because they do not arrest us; we do not see in them any reason for preserving them or for setting them apart. The profane stands over against the holy, not because it is sordid or "unclean," but because it is ordinary and harbors no mystery, nor calls forth the sense that beyond and beneath our life is a holy ground.

The basic relation between the holy and the profane may be summed up by saying that the holy provides the final purpose giving point and poignancy to all the details of profane existence, while the profane is the body of life and the medium through which the holy is made fully actual. Profane existence serves as a critical testing ground for the holy, in the sense that unless the holy takes historical form and becomes related to life in the world it may be dissipated in aesthetic enjoyment or contemplation that leaves life unaffected. The holy, on the other hand, is the standard for judging the profane since the holy provides us with a vision of what life should be, and thus reveals the extent to which mundane existence falls short of its ideal. The mutual involvement of the holy and profane is best understood by considering each as it might be if it existed all alone.

Profane life without the holy would be untouched by devotion to any but finite and limited objects—self, family, profession, nation—and such life would be without conviction about a final purpose for existence and devoid of a sense of dependence upon a transcendent source of existence. There would be no sense of the mystery of being; life would simply be given as one form of existence among others and, while life could well embrace the enjoyment of goods and values within the cycle of both nature and culture, it would not be viewed as the expression of a more than human purpose or power. Such visions of an ideal form of life as there would be would have to be constructed, in understanding and imagination, from the facts of natural existence. There would be no other source of information, so to speak, to illuminate human life and furnish insight into what man was "meant to be."

The holy without the profane, on the other hand, would become a sphere of pure "spirit" in which the transcendent holiness would be celebrated without concern for its embodiment in historical existence. Were the whole of life swallowed up in sacred existence, we would have a model of what the holy all by itself would mean. Religion would be the entire reality and profane life would have no being at all. Religion would remain in merely implicit form, there being no profane existence to give it actuality. If the profane without the holy means that life is bereft of spirit or depth, the holy without the profane would mean the cessation of life altogether.

There is a limit to the insight that can be gained by supposing what is contrary to fact. Actual life embraces both the holy and the profane and the question concerns neither one nor the other taken in isolation, but the proper connections between them.

The two have independent natures *vis à vis* each other in the sense that neither can be dissolved into the other, and yet they must be brought into some mutual relationship. The holy is not to be set entirely apart in a special sphere where it loses its critical power and where its judgment upon profane life is lost or nullified. On the other hand, the holy has to be set apart; it must not become too familiar or fall to the level of what is ordinary. That is, the attempt to interpret the holy as merely the "soul" or "spirit" of the profane in a way that does not allow for a due sense of awe in the presence of the holy is bound to fail. The holy stands over against the profane at the same time that it manifests itself in and illuminates the purpose of the profane. The crucial events of life in which the holy is present require special celebration through the ritual and symbolism of positive religion; if this does not happen, the holy gradually declines in significance and in power. The limit of this process is the profanation of life or, in terms more frequently used, the totally secularized society. It is impossible to maintain the holy merely as an idea or a general pervading spirit; actual celebration is required so that, insofar as the holy coincides with religion, religion must take on a positive and visible form in a cult and church. The church exists as the means of giving shape to the celebration of the holy. There is literally a life of religion, but it cannot exist merely alongside of profane life; the truth lies in interpenetration rather than co-existence.

Religious life, on the other hand, does not exhaust the whole of life; the belief that it does marks the basic flaw in the monastic conception. For the profane has its own being and autonomy over against the holy and does not exist merely to be swallowed up. There are natural structures and fulfillments in life, both individual and social, that are not to be understood solely through the idea of the holy. One can see this clearly in cultures where the preponderance of the holy has either prevented or greatly retarded the development of profane life. Such a state of affairs is no less distorted than one in which the profane constitutes the whole of life and the holy ground of existence is obscured.

Having considered the relation between the holy and profane existence, it is necessary to clarify the relation between what has been called the religious dimension of experience and the idea of God. The religious dimension involves viewing our life and experience as having a ground and a final purpose. The possibility of such a ground and a purpose first becomes explicit through experience of the crisis events and their disclosure of the holy depth of life. These experiences are occasions upon which man's capacity as a religious animal is realized, for at the crucial turning points in human life man becomes aware of actually attending to and wondering about his own being, about the mystery that, though he individually might not have been, he nevertheless is. At such times he is led to ponder the purpose of existence as such. The crucial times, moreover, force an awareness that man is a dependent being, that he is not self-sustaining, and that he needs to find an object of supreme worth to which he can devote himself if he is to achieve self-realization. This threefold awareness to which we are led represents, from the side of purely human experience, the material of the religious dimension. The events of crisis do not themselves constitute any resolution of the religious question, but merely provide the *occasions* upon which man discovers the meaning of the religious question and the urgency of his need for an answer. It is an error to suppose that the religious dimension of experience is itself positive religious faith, or that it is the "material" out of which the reality of God is, so to speak, constructed. To think in these terms would be to think of experience as somehow constituting reality instead of being a medium through which reality is disclosed.

There is, however, an essential connection between the religious dimension with its cycle of crucial events and the idea of God. The connection becomes manifest at the point where the sense of awe in the presence of the holy ground of life disclosed in the special occasions of life is grasped as concentrated in one supreme reality and identified with God. There is an asymmetry in the order of events. From a purely logical standpoint we cannot pass from the experience of awe and power to the

God who is disclosed in and through the special revelatory events that define the substance of Christian faith. The order must be reversed; the idea of the God in whom Christians believe must first be presupposed in order for the identification to take place. And indeed it is possible for a person to be overcome with a sense of awe and to raise the question of the ground and purpose of existence on these occasions without at the same time believing that the Christian God is present at all. But it does not follow that the crucial times at which the religious dimension of experience becomes explicit contribute nothing to an understanding of the idea of God. If belief in God in the religious sense is to make a difference in the conduct of life on the level of the profane, the meaning of that belief must be related to human experience in all of its dimensions. The reality of God from the religious standpoint means the answering of the question about the ground and purpose of human life. Failure to understand this point is a major factor in the perpetuation of merely conventional religion in which belief in God is either the fulfillment of a duty imposed by an institution or the inert belief that, in addition to all the finite things that exist, there is one more existent being called "God." If, however, the religious dimension of experience is understood and taken seriously, belief in God takes on new meaning. Belief in God then means belief in a reality of whose presence we are especially aware on the crucial occasions of life and it means a reality upon whom we depend for our being, our purpose, and our fulfillment.

To ignore the religious dimension of experience in favor of a wholly dogmatic approach to God through revelation is an error. The attempt to present God as a being who breaks into the world and human life entirely *ab extra* through sheer self-disclosure must always fail to convey to the would-be believer a proper understanding of the meaning of his belief. The meaning of God in religious terms—as distinct, that is, from the philosophical meaning—cannot be divorced from an understanding of the human situation out of which the question of God arises. If there were no concept of God, if the term "God" were but a name defined entirely in terms of a historic faith, there would be no point in attending to the general structure of human experience in order to understand how the question of God first presents itself. There are continuities in human life, spanning and overarching the many differences that distinguish people and nations from each other in different cultures and different regions of space. It is unlikely that the human predicament to which Christianity specifically addresses itself is unique to certain people. The *problem* of God presents itself in experience as determined by the universal structure both of the world and human life. The *resolution* of the problem is another matter; a particular understanding of God such as we find in the Hebraic tradition or in Christianity is, of course, dependent on the special media of disclosure or revelation that were actually involved; such revelation is a singular rather than a universal affair. And it remains so even when an attempt is made to universalize the revelation as being *the* answer to the human situation as such, and not simply a parochial belief confined to a time and a place. But howsoever unique a particular understanding of God derived from a historical religious tradition may be, there is also a generic idea of God, a concept of the reality that is the source, purpose, and fulfillment of existence. This concept is forced upon us in the course of our experience when we confront the question of our own being. Unless the idea of God as understood from the standpoint of Christianity (or any particular religion) is related to the question of God as it arises in our experience through the crisis events of life, there will be much confusion and a consequent failure on the part of religious people who profess belief in God in Christian terms to understand that the object of their faith is the one who ends the quest for a final purpose that is set in motion by life itself. Without an understanding of the relation between a particular faith in God and the dimension of experience out of which the generic problem of God arises, belief in God even of the most rigidly orthodox kind may become a mere adjunct to a person's life without that person ever understanding how his belief is related to his actual life both in its holy and in its profane aspects.

The religious dimension of experience, as has been repeatedly emphasized, does not of itself constitute God or the religious object. Experience is always a medium of disclosure, and its dimensions represent the different ways in which what is encountered comes to be understood. While the question of God may be seen as one that arises necessarily in the course of human experience, however, the reality of God understood in the concrete terms associated with the Hebraic and Christian doctrines of God takes us on to the idea of a particular divine disclosure or, in the traditional language of religion, *revelation.* It is essential that the *question* of God not be confused with the *disclosure* of God. The question of God does not answer itself, nor does the dialectic connected with the raising of the question within man's experience somehow resolve itself into an answer. For an answer it is necessary to turn to the possibility of revelation understood as disclosure from the transcendent side and as encounter from the side of man. The reality of God as distinct from the quest for God can be found only in the situation of encounter.

All forms of encounter have their appropriate locus, and for the encountering of God we turn to the crucial events of life, to the occasions when the holy becomes manifest. That the crucial events of life represent the disclosure of a concrete, divine reality, however, is not a feature that is to be read off the face of these events. As occasions for the disclosure of the holy, the crises of life remain merely indeterminate until further interpreted through some standard or normative disclosure of God. Such a normative disclosure belongs to the category of revelation; the problem of revelation is a central and inescapable one. But revelation or divine disclosure must not be set over against experience as if the latter were "natural" and the former "supernatural." For revelation represents a further development of the experiential matrix of religion, since experience is the only medium through which anything can be revealed to man.

Revelation is a category indispensable for religion, and its necessity is re-enforced by the fact that even in the development of natural or rational religion, as in the religio-philosophical movements of seventeenth-century Europe, for example, reason was regarded as a source of *revelation*. The reality of revelation raises new questions, not only in connection with the disclosure of God but in relation to the existence of God as such. For not only must we attempt to understand the meaning of God's disclosure, but we have to consider the recurrent uncertainties that arise in the mind of those who wonder whether there is any God at all. It is not too much to say that a rational and experiential religion maintains itself not in a static certainty that is unaware of doubt, but rather in a continual overcoming of the doubts that assail the revelation of God. For when God appears, the possibility of error and doubt also appears. The argument about God is a sign of this fact, and the arguments for God represent one way in which men have attempted to overcome doubt and to establish the reality of revelation on the far side of uncertainty.

III

The Disclosure of God and Positive Religion

Revelation or the disclosure of God in a medium of some sort is a phenomenon that must not be confused with theories about the nature of revelation as a way of knowing or as a ground of authority. Men placed their faith in an event or person as revealing the nature of God long before there existed precise statements about revelation as a channel of knowing distinct from and opposed to other ways of attaining insight into the nature of things. It is not generally understood that theories of the nature and authority of revelation are rarely, if ever, part of the normative basis upon which a religious tradition rests. This is eminently true of Christianity; for Christians, the figure of Christ is the final and normative disclosure of God and thus Christ is described as the revelation of the divine nature. But to say this is not to say that there is for all Christians one final and *ultimate theory of revelation* as a way of knowing. More often than not the development of the idea of revelation as a special kind of knowing has been the result of polemical discussion at a time when it is necessary to endow religious doctrines with a kind of authority over against skeptical criticism.

The disclosure of God, however, must be made intelligible, and an attempt must be made to interpret revelation in experiential terms. The disclosure of God is a relational affair; there are occasions upon which both the being and nature of God are made manifest, but if the manifestation is to be significant for the establishment of an actual religious tradition it must be a manifestation to a being capable of receiving what is thus disclosed. All that man knows and does takes place within the medium of experience; the manifestation of God as a reality transcending man and his experience is no exception to this general rule. Consequently, it is a mistaken opinion to believe that there is an essential incompatability between revelation and the approach to God through experience. Behind this view is the belief that revelation is a special way of knowing that is utterly different from, and wholly discontinuous with, human understanding as it comes into play on occasions when our concern is not with God but with other persons and things in the world. Revelation in the religious sense does involve something out of the ordinary, but it is unlikely that the manifestation of God would be intelligible to us at all if it happened only at times when man's capacities for experience and understanding are totally suspended. It is more likely that revelation would require, especially for its reception by the human mind, not the suspension of human capabilities, but rather their participation in an intensified form. Those who have interpreted revelation as a totally alien intervention into history, a message that falls into man's lap, as it were, from the outside, have usually been motivated by a desire to protect the divine mystery from the claims of an irreverent gnosticism. This aim is not without validity, but it can be accomplished in a way that is not self-defeating. Whatever is totally different from all we can experience and apprehend must be something that we neither experience nor apprehend and, far from calling this God, we should rather call it nothing at all. And indeed no one can consistently maintain such a view of revelation, for no matter how peculiar the disclosure of God may be we shall still require human thought, language, understanding, and experience in order to understand and interpret what has been disclosed. The only way in which the circle can be avoided is to claim that, in addition to the revelation of God, there is also a revealed or authoritative interpretation of what has transpired. But even this device fails, because once again human powers come into play at the point where it becomes necessary to understand and interpret the interpretation. There is no escape from the potential infinity of the process; there is no way in which human thought and experience can be excluded from the revelation situation.

On the other hand, acknowledging the role of the recipient in revelation does not mean the reduction of divine disclosure to purely human or natural proportions. For the disclosure of God is the disclosure of a reality transcendent of both man and his experience; such transcendence is not lost merely because we refuse to identify it with God's being "wholly other." Indeed all that we experience has its own independence and otherness over against us; the experience of God is no exception even though the divine transcendence differs from the exterior reality of finite objects. The peculiar character of revelation does not consist in the annihilation of man's capacity for understanding, but rather in a factor that makes no reference to man's ways of knowing at all, namely, in the fact that the disclosure of God takes place through a *historical* medium. Revelation occurs on certain special occasions—embracing both persons and events—that are capable of bearing the divine presence. These occasions are both historical and ultimate at the same time; they become fixed for a religious community as *the* normative revelation of God. These occasions and the content they disclose cannot be derived from any general theory of reality or from any theological system. Hence it is futile to ask whether, without such historical disclosure, we could have anticipated or "deduced" what becomes manifest on the occasions of revelation. Dependence on these historical occasions for the disclosure of God marks the boundary of human finitude and limitation. God is not in every sense "past finding out," but he is unattainable without the aid of the special occasions that provide the indispensable clue to him.

Revelation is always a relational affair; the special occasions are the times when the divine presence is disclosed through a medium,* but this presence has to be *received* in human experience. It is useless to speak of a "divine-human" encounter if the reality of the human pole is denied for fear of relativizing or subjectivizing God. Revelation cannot be divorced from the conditions under which it is received. It is not identical with those conditions, nor is its content constructed out of them. Revelation is a real disclosure of what transcends the one who

*In view of the fact that the term "medium" already has connotations that are likely to be confusing in the present context, it is necessary to make clear the sense in which the term is being used. To begin with, the term does *not* mean a medium in any spiritualist sense, as when someone who makes the claim that he is in contact with the "beyond" or with those no longer living, makes use of some "medium" to establish the contact. Nor is "medium" being used to mean the channels of communication we have in mind when we speak of "mass media" such as radio, television and the popular press. The term "medium" *is* being used in a sense most appropriate to the religious context; that sense can be made clear if we consider the major problem confronting every attempt to think about God. God, for the Judeo-Christian tradition, has never been understood as an object of sense—"no man has seen God at any time"—and therefore if God is to be apprehended in any fashion at all, this apprehension must be "mediated," which is to say that it must come through an "other." This is what is meant by theologians when they say that any supposed knowledge of God is also knowledge *of something else* at the same time. The "something else" is the *medium* through which God, who is not a sensible object, is to be known if known at all. When, for example, theologians have sought to know God *through the world* or *through a person* such as Jesus, or *through the Bible*, or *through the necessary truths of reason*, or *through history*, they have been appealing to various *media* through which it is possible that an otherwise non-sensible reality might be disclosed to man. Only the mystics, who seek to transcend all media of disclosure and expression, claim to apprehend God in and through himself without recourse to another. Christianity, though it includes a mystical strain within it, is not identical with mysticism; it has always viewed the disclosure of God as coming, not immediately, but through another or a medium—the person of Christ, history, Bible. These media—with the exception of the person of Christ which is discussed below, are not identical with the divine reality they disclose; they point to and disclose that reality in a way that is suited to their own natures. Thus the person as medium discloses the divine love; the Bible or book discloses the divine *Logos;* the historical order discloses the divine power and judgment.

receives it, but what is received and what that content means remains unintelligible apart from the medium of human experience. It is for this reason that man's interpreting mind cannot be suspended or deemed incompetent to receive the divine disclosure. On the contrary, the occasions of revelation are those upon which human powers and capacities are forced to their limit although their structures are preserved. Man has to receive what cannot readily be accommodated by ordinary patterns of thought and experience, and yet there is no other receptacle available. The mystery of God and the adventure of theology go hand in hand; in revelation man receives what he does not entirely understand, and yet he knows that he must try to interpret what he has received to the very limit of his ability. Whatever success he may enjoy in the process of understanding depends upon the inner connection between experience and the special occasions that find their place in a historical order. Revelation is not incompatible with experience because the special occasions of revelation are special occasions of encounter. The encounter is of an extraordinary sort by comparison with ordinary experience of persons and things, but it does not on that account pass entirely beyond the bounds of intelligibility, and for two reasons: first, there is continuity in experience enabling us to say that the encounter with God is *like* our encounter with finite persons and things, and second, the ground for belief in such continuity is found in the fact that revelation takes place through a historical medium for which experience in the sense of encounter is indispensable.

The vivid sense, shared by everyone who understands the role of revelation in establishing a historical religious community, that the disclosure of God must be something out of the ordinary, is misplaced if it means the mere displacement of human powers within the revelatory situation by some wholly unusual and "miraculous" form of communication. The truly unique character of divine disclosure is found, not in any disposition of the one who receives revelation, but in the nature of the disclosure itself—the crucial fact that it occurs through the medium of a temporal order made up of occasions that are unrepeatable. Man must wait upon these occasions as upon God's time for disclosure. Man must, to be sure, apprehend these occasions as such and he must interpret them with such light as he has and is given, but he cannot construct them from any general theory nor is he allowed to claim, once the occasions have taken place, that the insight they embody could have been gained in some other way, as if the historical medium were inessential. In revelation man encounters the Other of transcendence and, insofar as this Other is the source of man's being, the finitude of man is revealed at the same time. That finitude correctly interpreted, is not, however, the difference between a "natural" way of knowing and a "supernatural," but is rather the limit of *time*. Man is limited by time, not only in the obvious sense that he dies, that he came into being and passes away, but in the more profound sense that he must *wait upon* the special occasions of disclosure to discover the nature of God. When this limitation goes unacknowledged, the belief persists that human understanding and experience are essentially timeless and universal, unencumbered by the need to wait upon special occasions of disclosure. But even if we are able to grasp some truth that is independent of historical circumstances, we are limited by time in the knowledge of God.

The question naturally arises whether the special occasions of disclosure, involved as they are in parochial historical circumstances of time and place, exhaust our knowledge of God and, if this is the case, what contribution is to be made by our general experience of ourselves and the world derived from recurrent or repeatable occasions. Moreover, we need to know what role is to be played by other religious traditions with their claims to knowledge of God. Moses, Isaiah, Jesus Christ, and Paul belong to the special history of the Judeo-Christian tradition; each is bound up with the special occasions of revelation for that tradition and these occasions do not form part of the sacred history of, for example, Buddhists or the adherents of classical Hinduism. If God is to be regarded as the ground and source of all being, He must be related to the world and find expression therein; the recurrences of natural existence and the historical occasions of other religious traditions, therefore, will not be irrelevant to the process of divine disclosure. If, it is said, the basic clues to the divine nature are to be found in the special occasions of one religious history, it will not be obvious on the face of it how either knowledge of nature or the peculiar claims to knowledge of God advanced from other religious traditions can be taken into account. Shall they simply be denied on the ground that the disclosure of God through the special occasions of the Judeo-Christian tradition is final and exhaustive and nothing else is required? This solution has been advanced time and again in the course of Western history; it is a solution, however, that cannot be sustained. We cannot think at all without recourse to knowledge of ourselves and the world that is gained from sources other than that of the special occasions of revelation; moreover, the emergence of world problems and a new awareness of the reality of different religious traditions forces us to abandon parochialism and insularity. The stage in which the beliefs and practices of the non-Christian religions are seen as no more than bizarre chapters in the general history of civilization must be transcended. It has now become necessary to combine the truth contained in the approach to God through the special occasions of one religious history with the knowledge that has been gained through recurrent experience and the religious beliefs of other traditions. The key to the solution is found in the conditions that make interpretation possible. In order to apprehend the religious meaning of the special occasions, in order to apprehend, that is, what they disclose about God and how they are to be understood, we make use not only of our ordinary, secular knowledge, but also of the general concept of God as it has been derived from the religious dimension of experience which is universal. As we progress in understanding the meaning of our historical tradition, we are led to introduce comparisons with the other world religions and their ideas of God, ultimately arriving at the point where it is possible to consider objectively the shortcomings in our own religious insight that do not exist in other religions.

The fact that revelation is not self-interpreting turns the discussion back to the conditions for its reception, especially to the relation between revelation and the religious dimension of experience. As we generally stated at the outset, the relation between the two is that of the relation between *quest* and *fulfillment.* Revelation is the disclosure of what can be asked for but not attained wholly within the sphere of experience that finds its place within the profane world. What has previously been described as the religious dimension of experience is not the same as what must be called *positive religious faith.* For the latter we need more than a quest, we need revelation and the disclosure of a *concrete* God that makes possible the founding of a definite religious community with historical limits. From the religious dimension of experience and the grasp of the holy as distinct from the profane, we arrive at the concept of God and the meaning of the religious quest. We understand, that is, the possibility of a ground and goal of life and the need for a supremely worshipful Being. This possibility and this need belong to the structure of human life and experience generally; from consideration of the holy as a general category, however, we do not yet reach God in the concrete. In order to reach a concrete God something more is required. There is a gap between the religious dimension of experience and a definite conception of God, and it is for this reason that attempts to start with such a definite conception—the God of Christianity, for example—and then to translate this conception into the generalized holy for purposes of apologetics, always seem to be inadequate. Translation in this direction is bound to puzzle us because it appears as an attempt to ignore the gap. There is no completely logical transition from the holy as a general category to a definite conception of God such as that found in Christianity. The order may, however, be reversed; we may begin with the generalized holy as marking out a possibility and setting in motion a quest for the concrete God. But this quest is never fulfilled except in the events of revelation. Positive religious faith, as distinct from the religious dimension of experience, requires such a concrete God; without the definite idea of such a reality, there can be no established religious community, no structure for the religious life, no tradition to be interpreted, no formal locus for the celebration of the crucial events of the cycle of human life. Moving in the other direction, from the generalized holy in experience to the concrete God of revelation, enables us to see that, while involvement in the religious dimension of experience is necessary for all life, there is no clear necessity in the transition from that dimension to the concrete God who represents the fulfillment of the religious quest. The experience of the holy does not uniquely define the nature of God in the concrete, which is why there are many religious traditions.

The Christian understanding of revelation embraces the claim that there occurred certain events, and that certain persons played a part in them, which must be understood as disclosing the nature of God in virtue of the *presence* of God in those events and persons. The events in question are occurrences in the historical dimension, but they are not to be taken as merely occasions *upon* which God was disclosed, but rather as events *through* which the disclosure took place. The nature of the events and the persons is essentially connected with the religious meaning they bear. The crucial event for Christianity is the total life, including the death and spiritual continuation, of Christ. In that life we are to understand the presence of God and, consequently, the nature of God. Christianity, acknowledging its Hebraic heritage, does not regard the appearance of Christ as the *only* revelatory event, but accepts as well the revelatory occasions recorded and interpreted in the sacred history of the Old Testament. Thus the experiences of Moses and of the Patriarchs, of Isaiah, of Jeremiah, and, indeed, of the entire prophetic tradition are included within the complete cycle of revelatory occasions. Christianity, however, regards the figure of Christ as the *final* disclosure of God and thus as the norm by which to judge all other revelatory occasions.

Revelation means primarily the encounter of God through a medium. Three aspects of the revelatory situation call for elucidation. First, by a medium is meant a reality capable of bearing the divine presence and thus of standing *between* the God disclosed and the one who receives the revelation; second, by encounter is meant the experiential situation constituted by a reality presenting itself and an experiencing being equipped to apprehend that reality; third, the divine reality disclosed is made known in a twofold way—through the particular medium at hand and through the fact that a medium is necessary. God, that is, will be disclosed both as having a definite nature and also as being the kind of reality who makes himself known only through his presence in another.

In principle, any reality may serve as a medium of the divine presence, on the ground that God is related to all things and is able to express himself through them. In fact, revelation as it figures in an historical context is selective and exclusive. According to Christianity, God is disclosed in certain historical occasions, through certain persons, and, finally, through the special person of Christ. It is in this sense that we speak of history as the revelatory medium for Christian belief. Revelatory occasions take place as interpreted events within a historical order; their significance depends on the prior belief that historical time itself has a unified meaning as the chosen medium for the divine disclosure. Unlike traditions in which temporality is either denied or set aside as too transitory and insubstantial to express the divine nature, both Hebraic religion and Christianity see in the historical order the medium of revelation. For this reason, Christian theologians have always insisted on the placing of Christ in a historical setting; the One who provides the final manifestation of God is an historical being. This fact is not changed by the further fact that Christ needs to be interpreted in trans-historical terms in order to be grasped as the revelation of God. Christ is fully historical, but he cannot be understood entirely through historical categories.

A medium of revelation has the general character of being a reality in and through which God is present; it is also a reality that points beyond itself. The medium is not God, but that which discloses God. We see Moses on Mount Sinai, Isaiah in the temple, Christ on the cross; in each case we have a revelatory occasion disclosing the presence of God. In each case, however, it is necessary not to confound the event with God himself. The sign must not be mistaken for the reality it signifies; the sign reveals the reality, but only by pointing beyond itself to the divine being manifested in it. The natural tendency of man to overlook the distinction and to deify the media of revelation is attested to by the history of superstition throughout the ages. The doctrine that God hides himself at the same time that he discloses himself is meant as a warning against idolatry. If a man identifies the medium with God, he will fail to understand the presence of God in the medium; God will remain hidden. All media are, in the nature of the revelatory situation, finite and conditioned realities; the divine reality they disclose transcends them. Hence confusing one with the other leads to idolatry and not to revelation. Howsoever intimate the connection between the medium and the divine reality may be, there is always a gap between them; the medium is to reveal the presence of God but not to take the place of God.

The question that naturally arises is whether the distinction between the medium and God can be maintained in the crucial case of the central revelatory event of Christianity, the appearance of Jesus accepted as the Christ. At first it would appear that it is impossible to maintain the distinction at this point, for is it not said that Christ is identical with God and is it not claimed that Christ, as the final disclosure of God, is *the* presence of God without qualification or diminution? And yet Jesus prays to God and the Bible speaks of God being *in* Christ. The answer to the initial question, as is the case with most ultimate theological questions, has to be both yes and no. The task is to explain in what sense it is one or the other and how it is consistent to say both.

On the one hand, Jesus shares the character of medium with other persons and events in that he appears in the form of the servant who is obedient unto God, he constantly points away from himself to the one who alone is good and in whose name he comes, and he speaks of God under the image and office of the Father to whom he prays. Jesus reaches the apex of his role as medium at the point where he empties himself so that the divine will may be made manifest through his total obedience. On the other hand, Jesus differs from other media in that everything he does and says belongs to the divine disclosure and, as the final and normative revelation, he is the *full presence* of God, an embodiment that does not admit of degree. Being the full and final manifestation of God, Christ cannot, like other media, merely point beyond himself since he is the embodiment of the very being to which he would point.

Is it consistent, however, to make both of these statements at once? Christ, it would appear, is either one medium of disclosure like others, even though he is said to be the final one, or he is simply and undialectically identical with God, in which case describing him as a medium of disclosure becomes inappropriate or unnecessary. This dilemma could not be resolved were it not for a singular fact about a medium of revelation. The solving idea is implicit in the concept of a medium itself. It is the function of a medium of revelation to disclose God by bearing the divine presence but not by taking the place of God in the process. To perform its function, therefore, a medium must recede in order to disclose the reality to which the medium points. And yet the medium is not merely an occasion externally related to the reality disclosed; if that were so, the nature of the medium would make no difference to its meaning. In short, the medium must not, through its own nature, become a substitute for its meaning, and yet that nature cannot be entirely irrelevant to its meaning. The problem is found in connection with all the media of revelation, but it presents itself most acutely where Christ is concerned, for in that case the degree of internality existing between the nature of the medium and the divine nature is such that it cannot be surpassed.

Christ as the obedient servant provides the solving idea; his total obedience means at once the total presence and full revelation of God and the negation of himself in the process of disclosure. *A self-negating medium that reveals God in the very act of setting itself aside* is precisely the sort of reality required for solving the dilemma posed by Christ. The setting aside of the self and the total acceptance of the will of God in love and obedience is identical with the disclosure of God. The nature of the medium, or, since in this case the medium is a person, the mediating person, becomes identical with God without ceasing to be the means whereby God is made known to man. What Christ reveals is that God is to be understood as sacrificial love that exists in a concrete and personal form.

The revelatory situation is not exhausted in God and the medium of disclosure; it embraces those who receive the disclosure as well. Revelation, that is, must always be *to* and *for* someone. Those to whom the revelation is made and those by whom it is to be received must be able to apprehend it as such and interpret its meaning. For Christianity the reception is accomplished by individuals who exist within a special community of understanding. This community extends in two directions. As rooted in the past disclosure of God preserved in the records of the Old Testament, it is a *community of memory*. As rooted in the quest for the Christ who will make known the nature of God and make possible the ultimate communion of God and man, it is a *community of anticipation.* Those to whom God was revealed through the medium of Christ were those who had already known God, and who were thus looking for a final and total disclosure yet to come.

The Christian understanding of God as disclosed through a mediating person falls precisely between two opposite theories that have long been held concerning the knowledge of God. At one pole is the *mystical* view, according to which God is known *immediately* through an insight that can be attained by the purging of the self and by dialectical preparation of the mind. The ultimate goal of mystical preparation is to transcend all media of disclosure; media may play a role in preparing the self to receive the insight, but the aim of the mystical tradition in all religions is the final overcoming of all media, representations, and intermediaries by an immediate insight into God. The point was well expressed by the classical philosophical mystic, Plotinus, when he spoke of the "flight of the alone to the alone" and of the final insight as the apprehension of the One "with nothing in between." Christianity in its thought and experience can allow for an element of immediacy or a mystical element, but it would be an error to describe Christianity as an essentially mystical religion. For it does not accept the idea of "nothing in between" chiefly because of its commitment to the revelation of God through historical occasions. For Christianity every disclosure of God is also a disclosure of something else at the same time.

At the other pole is the *rationalistic* view, according to which knowledge of God is a matter of *inference* and never of immediate insight. Whereas the mystical way involves the immediate experience of God as the culmination of a process of preparation, the rationalistic approach excludes the idea that God can be experienced, but claims instead that God can be known as the result of an inference. Except for the ontological argument, which holds a peculiar place among the classical arguments for God, all the traditional arguments for God's existence, the cosmological arguments, the argument from design, the moral argument, furnish clear examples of the rationalistic approach. The starting point of the cosmological arguments is either the world in its immediate existence or some particular feature of the world, such as its design or the fact that it contains rational beings in it, and that starting point is regarded not as a medium of disclosure but rather as a fact expressed in a premise from which God is to be inferred. The thinking mind experiences the fact from which the inferential process sets out, but not the reality inferred; God is inferred to exist but is not experienced as such.

In the one case we have immediate experience of God in an essentially timeless unity that stands beyond all media and forms of expression, and who cannot be reached through inference; in the other case, we have an inferential process in which God, though known to exist, is not experienced but comes as a logical necessity and a "that which" that is required to make intelligible the existence of the world and certain of its features. The self is related to God only through an argumentative process of thought. The mystical approach holds fast to the reality of God and to the need for personal preparation and participation in religion, but its eschewing of argument results in the loss of a means of criticism, and its elevation of the self above historical life makes impossible the disclosure of a concrete God and the foundation of a historical religious community. The rationalistic approach holds fast to the logical necessity or intelligible aspect of God, and in so doing makes rational discussion possible, but it loses the personal and experiential aspect of the religious relationship because God as the terminus of inference never becomes a matter of experience in the sense in which the starting point of the argument is a matter of experience. The two polar approaches, though different in crucial ways, have an important feature in common: each sets aside the historical dimension of things in favor of what is timeless and universal. In the one case it is the elevation of the self beyond the limitations of its historical situation to the apprehension of a unity that is beyond all differentiation; in the other case it is the comprehension of a rational process that is, in principle at least, timeless in its universality and thus independent of particular historical circumstances. By contrast, the Christian understanding of revelation stands at once beyond and between the polar alternatives. It makes central precisely what is neglected in each, namely, history and historical occasions as media for the disclosure of God.

The belief that God is to be known through a medium leads at once to the marking out of a third alternative that is not reducible either to the total immediacy of mysticism or to the inferential process of rationalism. To say that God is revealed through a historical medium is to say that God is directly, but not immediately, experienced, and encountered rather than inferred. On the one hand, he is not immediately apprehended because he is known only in and through the medium; on the other hand, he is not inferred because he is *present* in the medium and the apprehension of that presence is something different from the logical process of inferring the divine existence by starting with some fact as a basic premise. The singular character of this view, especially the distinction between being *directly* and being *immediately* experienced, requires further explanation. No doubt the possibility of a new approach to the knowledge of God would have been envisaged sooner were it not for the widespread assumption that the alternatives of immediate experience and inferential argument are exhaustive. If this assumption should prove unwarranted, the way is open for the consideration of new possibilities. Why may there not be a way of apprehension that is not identical with either total immediacy on the one hand or inference employing universal concepts and logical rules on the other? The way of revelation through historical occasions furnishes an example of a third way; it involves both direct experience and rational interpretation but is not reducible to either alone. One is tempted to go further and claim that the way of historical revelation is necessary if we take seriously the nature of the God who is disclosed.

Immediate apprehension of an absolute sort is best suited for providing knowledge of immediate quality. It is clear enough that the colors, tastes, odors, and, indeed, all the qualities customarily described as sensory, can be apprehended only in immediacy. The color yellow is to be conveyed only through sight, and to a person who has never seen it there is no conceptual way in which the meaning of the term "yellow" taken as a color can be conveyed. On the other hand, the rationalistic approach to reality is best suited for apprehending the universal and repeatable features of things and the formal relations that obtain between the statements we make in expressing these features. The two extreme instruments of our knowing apparatus appear to be best fitted for grasping either singular quality at one pole or universal and recurrent characters of things at the other. The question naturally arises whether either of these instruments taken in isolation would be adequate for grasping a concrete unity such as an individual thing or person. An individual thing or person is neither an immediate quality nor a universal, and it would seem that unless we had other means of apprehending reality than those acknowledged by mysticism and rationalism we would find ourselves unable to know either persons or things. But we must go even further and consider the matter of knowing God. God is neither an immediate quality nor a universal character; would it not then follow that if immediate insight and conception plus inference exhausted our knowing equipment, no knowledge of God would be possible? The key to resolving this problem is furnished by asking how knowledge of an individual *self* is attained, for knowledge of the self is the most adequate model we have through which to understand the knowledge of God. The question as to how far and in what sense God can be said to be a self is one that need not be fully answered at this point. It is sufficient to point out that in the Christian understanding of God, the model and image of a self have played a central role; it is therefore legitimate to approach the problem by inquiring into the way selves are encountered and known.

The self, the individual person, encountered in experience is obviously neither an immediate quality to be known through immediate insight nor a universal character to be known through concepts alone. A self has precisely the character of being *directly present* in experience and thus of not needing to be inferred, and yet a self is not immediately known in encounter because it must express itself through various media that must be interpreted before their meaning is delivered. The parallel between the knowledge of finite selves and the disclosure of God through the medium of historical occasions and the person of Christ is very close, and thus it furnishes us with a means of insight into a relationship that might otherwise be opaque. If we can understand how a self can be directly present to another self and yet require a medium or form of expression through which disclosure takes place, we shall have some idea of what the revelation of God means.

The first point to be noticed is that the view which says that we encounter a person *first* as a collection of actions, spoken words, gestures, facial expressions, and other forms of behavior, and *then* infer that there is a person present needs to be reconsidered. On occasions where such behavior is encountered, a person is directly present in that behavior and expressing himself through it. The precondition for our taking spoken words, facial expressions, etc., as a sign of a center of purpose and intention, is that we already understand ourselves to be in the *context* of encountering and communicating with another person. There is no question of inferring an existent from evidence or behavior, because that evidence is intelligible only insofar as it is already taken to be the expression of a person directly present. If we attend to what actually happens when we encounter each other, we see at once that we never infer the existence of the other person. On the contrary, the other person is acknowledged as such at the beginning of the encounter. The problem that arises in connection with encounter between persons is not the *presence* (the "that") of the other person, but the discovery of *who* (the "what") he is, what he means to say, his character, his plans, purposes, and beliefs. Acknowledgment of this fact brings the discussion to the second point.

It belongs to the nature of a self to find expression. The medium of language is the indispensable element in the process. In confronting another self, I do not find myself in possession of a series of immediate insights into his character, his ideas, his aims and goals. That is to say that he does not present himself to me as a being whose personality can be *immediately* apprehended. In order for him to reveal himself, he must express himself through a range of media. In this sense even his actions take on the character of a "language" and become a channel through which the person reveals himself. When I encounter another person through various forms of expression it becomes necessary for me to receive these expressions in a significant way. I must interpret them as having some meaning whether they are regarded as conscious intentions to communicate or not; through interpretation I come to know not only what a person wants to say on a particular occasion, but I also learn something of his enduring character and general disposition at the same time. The fact that I do not have immediate access to another person makes it impossible for me to know him in a wholly immediate or intuitive way that would render interpretation unnecessary. It is not that we can dispense with direct experience, such as observing a facial expression or noticing a gesture of the hand; what is impossible is that one self should come to know and understand another without any medium at all or without the need for interpreting signs. The self expresses itself in and through the media, and yet transcends them at the same time since no one medium or occasion for expression exhausts the total unity of the self. Apart from media of expression, however, the self remains inaccessible.

In the Christian understanding of revelation, God stands to those to whom he is revealed in a relationship that is analogous to the situations in which two selves encounter each other. There are, of course, differences between the two cases and hence we say that they are *like* each other but not that they are identical. The disclosure of God, that is, is not the same as one more encounter between finite selves, but the similarities are sufficient to warrant the belief that if we attend to one situation we can gain some understanding of the other.

Revelation in the Christian view means that there are occasions when the nature of God is disclosed—occasions, that is, when God is present in certain mediating elements. These elements function as signs, and as such require reading or interpreting by the one who receives them. Interpreting has always been regarded as the classic task of prophets and theologians. In the Old Testament tradition where the prophetic office was highly developed, the prophet is not, as in the popular meaning of the term, primarily a soothsayer or fortune teller; he is described instead as an interpreter, one who "discerns the signs of the times." He is often characterized as—and indeed the Greek term means—one who *speaks for* or *in the name of someone else.* "Thus says the Lord . . ." is the familiar preamble to prophetic speech, and it is followed by an interpretation of an experience or prophetic vision taken as a medium for disclosing God's will or word for man. The writers of the New Testament books, although they cannot be called prophets in the classical sense, carry on the tradition of interpreting by recording events and providing commentary. St. Paul carries the task further and initiates an explicitly *theological* reflection aimed at interpreting the meaning of Christ, his office, his nature, and his disclosure of God by the use of consistent concepts pointing in the direction of a theological system. The final chapter in the interpretative process is still being written; it includes the extensive record of theological interpretation that reaches from the Church Fathers, both Greek and Latin, to the present day. Although many different theological systems have appeared in the long course of Western history, the task of the theological interpreter has ever been the same—to interpret the signs and to say what the media of disclosure, especially the disclosure in Christ, convey about the nature of God.

Christianity presupposes the Old Testament record of the divine disclosure, and, indeed, the New Testament writers use this understanding of God as a framework within which to interpret the figure of Christ, even though Christ is believed to transcend this framework at the same time. The Hebraic tradition from beginning to end expresses the firm conviction that God can be known only through a medium of some sort. Three media were made central; they are clearly distinguishable and yet they remain in living connection with each other. First, and most important, is the holy or prophetic *person* who is called to perform the work of mediation. Within the context of Hebraic religion, with its powerful emphasis on the ethical principles that should govern the conduct of persons in community, the task of the holy person centered largely in interpreting the divine will to the community of believers. Thus Moses, forever the crucial figure of the Hebraic tradition, is the one who conveys the divine will in the form of the law that defines the total religious and moral structure of human life and at the same time discloses a God who is majestic, who not only demands a total devotion but also a clear rejection of all other gods or idols. The prophetic persons, Isaiah and Amos, for example, interpret the ancient law, through the medium of historical situations and events, indicating its further implications for both men and nations.

It is important to notice that these holy persons perform functions in the process of disclosure, not as individuals *in* whom God is present, but rather as men *to* whom God appears as in a mediating situation. Following the ancient legends, God appears to Moses in the burning bush and on the holy mountain, and he appears to the prophetic figures in the form of visions and object lessons that can be understood only in connection with the historical events of their time. Although the personality and insight of the holy persons play an important role in the fulfilling of their office, the disclosure of God does not come about as the result of the presence of God in their own being, instead it is the divine presence in the historical events and the pattern in those events that constitutes the medium. The function of the holy persons in revelation is properly that of mouthpiece and interpreter; the historical occasions or special events that are the expression of the divine will, and it is the task of the prophetic persons to say what these occasions reveal concerning the nature of God.

Historical occasions and *pattern in history* represent the second medium of disclosure in the Hebraic understanding of revelation. Some commentators have exaggerated the contrast between the Hebraic emphasis on history as a medium of divine disclosure and the speculative approach of the Greek philosophers to problems concerning the nature of God. No exaggeration is necessary in order to make the basic point, which is that the Hebraic writers saw a linear pattern in history and, more important, they saw historical time as a reality substantial enough to be a medium of revelation. Quite apart from the historical question of the Greek view of history being basically cyclical in comparison with the linear view found in the Old Testament writers, the important consideration is whether this positive evaluation of time and historical order does not contrast sharply with any view that sees history as either illusory or too insubstantial to be a medium through which the nature of God can be disclosed. In Biblical religion, history functions as such a medium in a twofold sense; individual historical situations and occasions are seen as bearing the divine presence in the form of judgment or deliverance, and the course of history as a whole, the story of salvation, is understood as expressing the divine plan or Providence that is ultimately the final purpose of God in creating the world.

Historical occasions as a medium of disclosure exhibit clearly the revelatory situation as one in which God is present but not immediately known as such. The presence of the medium precludes any direct intuition or insight into the divine nature; that nature is made manifest through another and the other takes the form of historical events and tendencies of development (which is precisely what is meant by "patterns" in history) that must be regarded as signs of the divine presence. Such signs do not bear their meaning on their surface; they must be read or interpreted. The presence of God, however, is not inferred from historical events after the fashion of a cosmological argument; it is rather that God is encountered and known through these events as a reality present in power and will. The question of the right or warrant for viewing such events as expressions of a reality transcending them is one that belongs to the critical evaluation of revelatory media and not to their actual functioning in the religious situation.

The third medium in which the Hebraic religious tradition found the presence of God is the order and arrangement of nature. There existed in the Hebraic consciousness a strong sense of the consistency of the natural world as the expression of the divine will and understanding. The later Psalms, for example, are filled with poetic utterance giving voice to belief in the presence of God throughout the entire range of natural phenomena. The calling forth of all finite things from the deep shows the force of the divine Word which is at once an expression of consistent plan or purpose and of power to bring that purpose into being. God expresses his nature through the order of natural existence; his presence in that medium has to be discerned by those who have understanding. There is no hint of an inferential process from the created things back to their cause, although language implying power is frequently used; it is rather that the presence of God is discerned in the creation since that creation is a medium of expression. The analogy is with a centered or purposive reality expressing itself in its works, rather than with an argumentative process that sets out from given facts and explains those facts by invoking an ultimate ground for them. This point can be seen most clearly in the well-known "answer" to the riddle of evil in existence that comes out of the whirlwind to Job. Job's inability to understand how the existence of God can be compatible with the presence of evil and injustice in the world is not overcome by an argument to the effect that the order of nature requires God for its ground. On the contrary, the writer takes for granted the presence of God in that order at the same time that he describes that order as a mystery that surpasses human knowledge. Quite apart from the resolution to the problem of evil, which, as is generally agreed, the Book of Job does *not* provide, the aim of the writer is not to prove the reality of God, but rather to overwhelm Job with a sense of wonder at the presence of God in the meticulously planned structure of nature. Nature is not a datum to be made into the first premise for an argument; nature is a medium in which God is present in both form and power. As a medium it is a means whereby the disclosure of God is made possible. God is directly present to the believer in the order of nature but he is not immediately apprehended because nature is a sign or medium of expression and must be interpreted as disclosing a reality that transcends it as its creator and sustainer.

The joint working of the three media—holy persons, historical events, and the natural order—leads to the normative disclosure of God upon which the Hebraic tradition was founded. God appears as the supreme object of devotion, demanding nothing less than the full or wholehearted response of those who discern his presence in the signs. He appears as the creator of all things and as the law-giver who marks out the ground and goal of human existence as well as the principles that are to govern the relation between man and man. God appears as the Word and power controlling the historical process, the Lord of time whose presence can be discerned in the turning points of history for those who have learned to read the signs.

At one crucial point the Old Testament disclosure of God points beyond itself to a new kind of medium. In the book of Isaiah there appears the idea that a person in the form of the suffering servant can in some special way make clear the nature of God. Such a person would be similar to the holy persons as media of disclosure, but different at the same time. Whereas the holy persons were interpreters of the divine without themselves embodying the divine, the suffering servant is to be in some special and unique way the presence of God manifested throughout his being and his historical existence.

The turning point in the history of religion that is marked by the birth of Christianity out of the Hebraic tradition is found in the conviction that the historical figure of Jesus is to be regarded as that special and unique disclosure of God, that final manifestation of the divine nature to which such writers as Isaiah and Jeremiah point. In the New Testament writers the historical medium of revelation centers entirely on the one person who is taken to be the unique being in which the nature of God is made manifest. The tradition of revelation through the historical medium is preserved, hence the Christian theologian has always sought to maintain the true manhood of Christ as an historical being over against Docetic and Gnostic interpretations that would deny genuine historicity. The logical pattern of revelation is repeated; there is the divine reality to be disclosed, there is the medium of disclosure, and there is the interpreter who reads the meaning of the disclosure in terms of the medium.

The Christian view is that the total being and person of Christ, embracing his life, death, and continuation in the form of the spiritual body or church, represent *the* revelation of God. The claim that Christ is the final manifestation does not mean the negation of what went before and was accepted within the biblical tradition as valid disclosure of God; it is rather the fulfillment of that tradition. The very expectation of one who is to fill the office of Messiah or Christ depends on previous understanding of God derived from the Old Testament tradition. The Hebraic understanding of God thus forms the framework within which Jesus is initially interpreted as Christ. Without the existence of a community of anticipation there would have been no basis for determining a quest for one who functions as reconciler or redeemer. The anticipating community does not invent, but rather discovers the Christ in encounter; in performing the task of discovery the anticipating community becomes an essential condition within the revelatory situation. Encounter, as was previously made clear, is a relational affair, and that encounter which is revelatory requires not only a medium of disclosure but also experiencing beings who receive the disclosure and who understand how to interpret it.

Christ discloses the divine nature as one of sacrificial love endowed with the power to reconcile man to himself by overcoming the burden of guilt that follows from our awareness of the gulf between what man ought to do and be in terms of the divine law and what he actually is and does in terms of historical action and life. God is made known as a spiritual reality—the αγάπη that no man can create because it must be given from beyond man—who takes part in the cycle of human existence under historical conditions and who thus becomes directly related to the world that is to be recovered from its distortions and self-destructiveness. The organic unity of love, of purpose, of understanding, and of power disclosed in the one who bears the office of the Christ suggests that selfhood and personality are the most appropriate terms with which to characterize God from the Christian standpoint. The history of Christian thought embraces a long and intricate discussion about the question, posed in the language of Thomas Aquinas, "Whether the term 'Person' can be said of God?" and at present there is difference of opinion as to the answer. For some, God is nothing if not a person; for others, the literal ascription of personality to God is regarded as a crudity that must result in the reduction of God to the status of one being besides other beings and finally to the transformation of God into a finite reality. Howsoever this question is to be resolved, one fact remains clear: the disclosure of God in the figure of Christ points to an individual reality, spiritual in character, and including within its own nature capacities that are analogous to a self as known to us in human experience. The philosophical account of what it means to be a self, especially *the* self who is the unique, divine reality, may have to be accomplished by means of concepts such as being, intention, action, identity that are removed from direct experience and occupy a place in a comprehensive ontological theory, but there is no getting away from the fact that free, conscious, centered individuality is implied in the final disclosure of God in the Christian understanding.

The figure of Christ has always meant the disclosure of God in two aspects; they may be called the concretely religious and the universally philosophical. In the former aspect, Christ is the manifestation of God in the form of the Messiah answering to the purely religious quest for a source of power able to overcome the guilt of man and the self-destructive character of the human will to deny God and establish human freedom as the ultimate norm. The Messiah discloses God as the sacrificial love reconciling man to God and to himself. In the second aspect, Christ is the manifestation of God as the universal *Logos* of all being, the Word, the rational form and the intelligible plan that at once marks out the pattern of all things and stands as the fulfillment of the quest for cosmic rationality. The classic Christian faith embraces both these aspects; on the one hand, it stresses the historical particularity of the person whose mission it was to fulfill the religious quest by sacrificing himself that the love of God might be revealed; on the other, the same person is understood as universal *Logos* without which nothing created was made or established. That both aspects are found together in original Christian teaching is more certain than is any account of the manner in which they can be synthesized. No final synthesis has ever held sway within Christianity, and few, if any, theologians have been able to sustain an equal emphasis on each aspect. The religious aspect marks the line taken by theologians from Paul through Augustine and Bernard to Luther and, in the present day, to Barth, while the philosophical aspect has been uppermost in the development of theology from the Alexandrian theologians through Anselm and Thomas, to Hartshorne and Tillich on the current scene. Both aspects have powerful roots in the tradition and neither can claim to be "more basic" than the other.

Insofar as it is one God who is disclosed, it is essential that the two aspects be seen as compatible with each other and thus as more than externally related. Their coherent togetherness is best understood in terms of their interpenetration; the religious mission of the Messiah has to be seen as a *Logos*, as a word of life that is intelligible, and the philosophical mission of the *Logos* has to be seen as a particular truth about man and his destiny that intervenes in concrete human life with power to heal and transform. Each aspect shares the nature of the other; the religious aspect takes on philosophical character at the point where the Messiah is seen, not only as a concrete historical being, but as the bearer of an intelligible word about God, man, and the norm of human life; the philosophical aspect takes on religious character when the *Logos* is seen, not only as a truth with universal validity, but as a particular, concrete truth that intervenes in human life and has a practical power to recover life from its self-destructiveness.

The definite, historical disclosure of God means a transcendence of the religious dimension of experience and of the religious quest in the direction of positive religion. The disclosure of God, in virtue of its relational character, at once requires and establishes a religious community. In the first instance it is the community of those who receive the disclosure and become related to God both in their acceptance of the revelation and in their effort to understand what it means. Once established, the community becomes the locus of a positive faith which means, for those who acknowledge it, the fulfillment of the religious quest and the passage beyond the concern for the holy in generalized terms to *the* God beside which there can be no other. As the disclosure becomes clearer and more definite the community becomes more sharply defined and the positive religious framework more elaborate. The basis for the community and its being is the spiritual relation that obtains, on the one hand, between God and the members and, on the other, the spiritual relations that obtain among the members themselves. The community is rooted in the disclosure of God, but that disclosure involves as well those who receive it and the acknowledgment of each individual when he personally accepts the specific revelation of God to which the community testifies. The disclosure can never be a wholly "objective" transaction in the sense that its character as disclosure is retained entirely independently of its reception by an anticipating community. Jesus, for example, was contemporaneous with and was encountered by many persons for whom he was *not* the final disclosure or manifestation of God; in the case of those persons the conditions of reception were not fulfilled. On the other hand, we must not say that the disclosure is totally dependent upon, or wholly resolved into, its reception. To say that the revelatory situation is a relational affair is precisely to stress the necessity of both sides—a reality disclosed and its reception within a community of acknowledgment or faith.

In order to preserve its own foundation, the community determines that the disclosure of God will be cast into the form of a written record containing an account of the revelatory events and their interpretation. This record is gradually expanded, expressed in systematic and consistent form through an extensive dialectical process. The resulting theology expresses the faith and marks out the limits of the religious community, thus giving shape to the positive religion it represents. The contrast between natural and revealed religion that played so large a part in the religious thought of the late seventeenth and eighteenth centuries contains an important element of truth. Revealed religion was identified as *historical* and as rooted in a historical disclosure of God as over against the natural religion that was supposed to be independent of historical limitations. No identifiable religious community was associated with the natural religion as such. The reason is that such a community is found only in connection with a historical disclosure of God and the community that receives it. The disclosure of God through nature understood as a universal possession, and through universal truths derived from reason or from beliefs taken to be common to all religions, forms no definite community of faith. The adherents of natural religion were, so to speak, without a community of their own and hence were forced to graft their beliefs onto the existing Christian community, producing in the end a deistic form of Christianity. Some abandoned religious practice within the framework of the church altogether and thought of themselves as members of a purely intellectual community free from ritual and organized religion. The entire development is important for the light it throws on the connection between a historical or specific disclosure of God and the founding of a positive religious faith in a historical community of believers.

The so-called natural religion represents a form of the generalized holy, but it has no roots in a specific disclosure of God and it does not involve acknowledgment of special revelatory events. Just as the generalized holy cannot be determined by a date in time and a place in space after the fashion of historical disclosures of God, so the intellectual community of those who acknowledge only the generalized holy is without a date and a place; it exists only as a state of mind and as an acknowledgment of beliefs held in common, but there is no worship of a structured sort, no sacred organization of either space or time and no loyalty to a historical community that lives in the vicissitudes of history. Positive religious faith expressed in a visible community takes us beyond the confines of the generalized holy: such a community can come into being only through a concrete or particular disclosure of God.

Howsoever successful we may be in finding models and analogues in experience for the revelatory process, the question must always arise about the possibility of subjecting the disclosure of God to critical appraisal. The question is this: does revelation have any warrant or ground upon which it rests, or is it to be accepted as a communication *ab extra* that must be received but not questioned? The problem was expressed in a most arresting way by Royce through what he called the "paradox of revelation." A disclosure of God is received and the question is raised whether it bears on its face any marks that enable us to assess its validity. The paradox arises at the point where we see that the criteria by which we would evaluate or judge the disclosure must be supplied by the disclosure itself; the recourse to revelation implies that man, through the use of his resources alone, is unable to apprehend the concrete God who alone is worthy of worship. But if the marks by which the disclosure of God is to be tested are themselves delivered in that disclosure, we seem to be caught in a circle. Royce proposed the example of a draft drawn on a bank account; the authenticity of the check can be determined by comparing the signature on its face with the standard signature of the account holder on file at the bank. The analogy is illuminating because it nicely exposes the dilemma; if a particular disclosure of God is a draft on the truth, its authenticity must be checked, to carry out the figure, with the divine signature. That signature, however, is given only in the disclosure itself. Does this mean that all revelation must be self-authenticating or grounded in immediate intuition or in some form of self-evidence? The answer to this question can be given only by attending to the relation between the disclosure of God and the medium through which disclosure takes place. The view that revelation must take place through a medium precludes an easy appeal to self-evidence and intuitive insight. Is there a theory of the relation between the medium and the meaning it discloses that can successfully resolve the paradox of revelation?

IV
Doubt and Living Reason

The interpretation of the religious concept of revelation in terms of experience furnishes a context for resolving the "paradox of revelation." From the critical standpoint, the resolution of this paradox consists in the insight that revelation, while indispensable, nevertheless needs to be made intelligible in terms of experience. The acceptance of revelatory claims is not then the acceptance of an external authority, but acknowledgment of the intrinsic intelligibility of what is revealed about God. Dogmatic religion takes its stand on the self-authenticating claim of revelation and thus refuses to acknowledge the validity of any outside standpoint from which revealed truth might be criticized. Critical or rational religion cannot follow this path; first, because it recognizes not only the fact but the necessity of criticism, and second, because rational religion is rooted in the belief that religion is intelligible and that it can maintain itself only in and through criticism.

It may, however, be objected that if revelation can be criticized or stands in need of support from beyond itself, what need is there to appeal to it at all? The parallel between the special experiences of revelation and the general nature of experience helps to answer this perennial question. We interpret and criticize what is encountered in experience without thereby abandoning experience as a touchstone or standard. We examine and sift experience, and subject it to critical tests, without feeling the need to dispense with experience altogether. Why may not the same be true of the experiences of revelation? Suppose revelation were indispensable, but *not* immediately authoritative. If that were the case, revelation would stand in need of *indirect* critical support; revelation would remain indispensable but it would not have to be dogmatically accepted.

From the critical standpoint, revelation is not an immediate and final solution, but rather a problem to be resolved. The claim of revelation is made to rational beings capable of doubting and ever searching for ways to overcome their doubt. The history of philosophical theology in Western thought has been a history of dialectical interpretation and rational appraisal of the religious content; critical theology has never been a mere catalogue of the articles of faith. On the contrary, the volumes of discussion described, sometimes scornfully, as the dusty disputes of theologians, actually represent a massive critical dialectic aimed at showing the intelligibility of revelation against doubt and uncertainty. Such dialectic has frequently focused on the central reality to which revelation points—the reality of God. For rational religion the argument about God is unavoidable, although it is not necessary to understand this "argument" solely in terms of the traditional attempts to "prove" the existence of God. One of the problems to be resolved is whether intelligibility must mean "proof" and how such proof could be expected to function in the religious context. The critical discussion or argument about God arises from the insight that revelation is not immediately authoritative and that it can always be questioned. The problem is to determine how the dialectical attempts that have been made to answer critical questions about revelation are themselves related to the revelation they would support. In short, how is the argument about God related to the experience through which revelation comes? In order to answer this question it is necessary to consider more closely the nature of doubt in the religious situation and the type of critical reflection through which doubt may be overcome.

For the critical mind, and especially for one steeped in the philosophical tradition, any account of religion which makes knowledge of God ultimately a matter of direct experience must seem inadequate. For critical discussion always carries with it the demand for conclusions which are *rationally compelling* in the sense that the thinker grasps the logical force of the argument and is carried along toward the conclusion, having throughout a sense of rational constraint and of comprehension. The curious fact is that when our analysis leads to the conclusion that the having of certain encounters or direct experiences is more important than apprehending that a given conclusion "follows from" a given premise, a feeling of disappointment is likely to result. The philosopher is inclined to feel himself closer to *knowing* than to *having*, closer to thought than to experience, so that no matter how essential the role of experience may be, the philosopher demands that critical reason shall determine how that experience is to be interpreted.

Charles Peirce saw this problem clearly, and his solution is one that demands attention. In assaying the religious dimension of life, Peirce came to the conclusion that apprehending God is a matter of direct experience; he was unwilling, however, to put his conclusion forward as a matter of dogmatic assertion or intuitive certainty. Instead he offered what he called an argumentation * intended to support his thesis that no purely deductive argument will suffice to prove the reality of God (if the argument is really about God). Peirce was thus attempting to give *rational* support to the thesis that the reality of God is not a matter of direct proof, but that it is instead, as he called it, a direct

* It must be noted that Peirce distinguished between an "argument" and an "argumentation"; see *Collected Papers of Charles Sanders Peirce*, Eds. Charles Hartshorne and Paul Weiss (Cambridge, 1931–35), Vol. VI, sec. 456, 457: "An 'Argument' is any process of thought reasonably tending to produce a definite belief. An 'Argumentation' is an Argument proceeding upon definitely formulated premises."

perception. Even the theory that direct perception has the priority over deduction is set forth as having a rational ground and thus as indirectly proved.

Despite the tension between direct experience and the way of proof, a critical approach requires that no solution be accepted at face value and that every proposal, regardless of its nature, be considered dialectically and in relation to the rational grounds upon which it rests. Since the present chapter proposes to consider the argument about God or self-dependent being * we want to treat the classical attempts to prove the existence of God and especially to see how these proofs are related to experience. It is essential to know whether these attempts imply that experience may be dispensed with, on the assumption that the proofs proceed from idea to idea without the need of encounter, or whether they actually contain direct experiences as part of the content of ideas through which the argument moves. As a general introduction to the proofs themselves it will be helpful to consider the situations and motives out of which they emerge. In this way the religious significance of proof itself may be grasped and its relation to faith made clear. It is not enough to analyze, accept, or reject the proofs as they appear; it is necessary as well to understand the religious situations out of which they arise and to appraise them in accordance with their aims and an understanding of exactly what proof may be expected to accomplish within the sphere of religious belief.

Critical questioning concerning the reality of God presupposes that direct belief in or conviction concerning this reality has been lost, or shaken by some uncertainty. The very hint of proof is a sign that some form of *doubt* has entered into the re-

* Most frequently in the past, God has been interpreted metaphysically as "independent being," with the result that the stress falls upon transcendence of the world and it becomes difficult to make intelligible God's relation to man and the cosmos. To speak instead of "self-dependent being" places the emphasis upon the divine nature directly and then leaves open the question of how a self-dependent being would be related to the world and to man.

ligious situation. Doubt and uncertainty *as they appear in religion* must be clearly understood, otherwise it remains uncertain how doubt can be removed or rendered powerless through the discovery of rational grounds for faith. In the past many philosophers have devoted serious attention to the phenomenon of doubt, and its philosophical importance has been established beyond question.* There has, however, been the tendency to view the phenomenon in the most narrowly *cognitive* or theoretical context and thus to consider it only insofar as it is a stimulus to theoretical inquiry or a starting point on the road to fully developed science. The peculiar meaning of doubt in the religious situation has often been neglected, as has also the *conative* side of uncertainty, that sense of doubt which is more closely connected with the will and purpose of the self than it is with precisely formulated theoretical questions. The person of whom we say, "his heart is not *in* his work," or "he does not believe *wholeheartedly* in what he says," is a person in doubt, but this doubt is of a different and more elusive kind than the critical or scientific doubt that prompts carefully formulated questions. The doubt from which science is born guides the quest for information; the uncertainty that haunts religion is stilled only by inspiration and confidence.

Religion embraces doubt in both of its principal forms, a doubt which has a *cognitive* root and one which has a *conative* basis. The two poles embraced by doubt may be called the *conceptual* and the *feeling* poles. At the feeling pole, doubt is vague in large measure because it is so deeply imbedded in the self, or, conversely, because the self is so deeply involved in it. The self feels an opposition within itself resulting from a sense of incongruity or incompleteness. The incongruity need not have reached the level of explicit formulation as logical opposition or contradiction, although reflection and analysis will usually show

* For many philosophers the entire nature and function of reason consists in its power to overcome doubt and to establish settled belief on the far side of uncertainty.

that such an opposition or contradiction is present. Felt incongruity may be illustrated through may familiar experiences; it is present when our sense of justice is outraged by some action or event which seems to us wrong or unjust; it is present when we are ill at ease because we have failed to complete a task to our satisfaction or when we experience the pangs of conscience which are the felt incongruity and discrepancy between what we know ourselves to be or to have done in fact and the power of the ideal which has a claim upon us. In all these cases the self is concerned and deeply involved with its own being; the self is in an unstable state, a state of uncertainty, insecurity, and doubt because the situation is incongruent or discrepant; the self is not at peace with itself and its world. The feeling pole which reveals the concern of the self for the object that is in doubt is present in all sincere questioning. But this feeling cannot exist entirely apart from the conceptual pole, which introduces some theoretical distance into the situation, for without interpreting ideas there can be no incongruity or uncertainty at all. The important point, however, remains: there is a genuine feeling pole in religious doubt and it involves the moral and esthetic capacity of the self. Moreover, religious doubt touches the basic attitude, orientation, and volitional capacity of the self because the manner in which a person responds to his situation and acts is primarily a result of how settled and firm he is in his basic convictions about God, his world, and himself. Life is disrupted as long as it remains filled with felt oppositions, when the self is continually aware of a discrepancy or imperfection involving its own being or the ultimate certainties from which it lives.

Even the vaguest sense of incongruity, however, rests ultimately upon an opposition of ideas or concepts. Careful reflection is often necessary to reveal the presence of these ideas, and that is precisely the point at which the conceptual pole enters in. All doubt has its conceptual foundation; it is because of this fact that the cause of doubt can be grasped and the means of dispelling it can be made clear. At the conceptual pole, doubt becomes a matter of explicit question and answer; it ceases to be merely a matter of feeling and becomes instead a matter of directed inquiry, whether of an empirical or dialectical sort. When the basis of doubt is grasped, the incongruity or contradiction in the situation emerges, the difficulty is located, and the one who would remove doubt must find a way of meeting the difficulty so as to deprive of it its disruptive force.

Both of these poles may be illustrated in the religious situation outlined in the Book of Job. Many treatments of the Book of Job have failed to see the full significance of this profound writing because they have viewed it in too narrow a way, taking it merely as the case of a man who was determined to preserve his own right to raise critical questions about God instead of accepting dogma without query.

Job's doubt and the uncertainty of the situation is twofold; it not only embraces his explicit critical questioning and testing of one of the cherished beliefs of the Wisdom conception of God, but also it shows the depth of his personal involvement in a cosmic incongruity before which he feels his own uncertainty and despair. At the conceptual pole, the doubt of Job is based upon his explicit awareness of an inconsistency between his own individual fortune in the world and the conception of God in which he was reared. According to that conception those who are in right relations with God do not suffer as he was made to suffer. Job's doubt grew out of his explicit grasp of the contradiction involved; his integrity consisted in nothing more than his honest refusal to follow the advice of his comforters and remove the contradiction by an *ad hoc* theory. Such explicit dialectical discussion as the Book of Job contains is directed to the problem of removing Job's critical doubts concerning the reality of the God in which the wisdom tradition had come to believe.

Were this the whole of the matter, however, the Book of Job would be nothing more than a critical discussion dressed up in highly dramatic and rhetorical form. The fact is that Job's doubt and uncertainty has another side; his uneasiness consists in a felt opposition deeper than could be removed or overcome by any dialectical argument. Job's uncertainty concerns not only his quest for understanding, for explanation, but his need of courage, of inspiration, and of a proper attitude or *stance* * with which to confront and overcome the misery of his life. It is wrong to suppose that Job's doubt and uncertainty would be completely overcome if only a cogent and defensible solution to the problem of evil were forthcoming, for his doubt is not of a wholly conceptual character and it does not spring entirely from the demand for explanation. Job wants inspiration and courage as well as understanding; he looks for a purpose for a life which, as he says, had its way hid, and he hopes to achieve within himself an inner security which will make continued existence possible within a perplexing and frustrating world. It is important to notice that Job does not reject the arguments and reasonings of his comforters merely because they contain logical flaws; he finds those arguments inadequate because they have an air of *inappropriateness* about them. The uncertainty and doubt he is trying to overcome is not to be dealt with by argument alone. It is not that the arguments of his comforters are nonsensical, but that they are inappropriate for stilling a certain aspect of Job's doubt—the doubt and uncertainty surrounding Job's *being* in the world, his attitude toward his lot, and his courage and endurance in facing it. Another way of expressing the point is to say that rational explanation aimed at removing Job's conceptual or clearly formulated doubt would not necessarily be equally effective in coping with his felt opposition or the uncertainty concerning his own ability to survive in a world so filled with disappointment and suffering. Within the religious situation, the doubt that reaches explicit formulation can only be overcome by the attainment of settled *belief*, whereas the doubt and uncertainty springing from the feeling pole and touching the being and basic orientation of the self in the world can be overcome

* See pp. 102–3.

only by *conviction* or a firm sense of courage which can withstand defeat. Genuine religious *faith* embraces both of these elements—belief and conviction—and the two are held together in faith as the *cognitive* and *conative* sides of the full religious life.

Both aspects of doubt must be taken into account because both are of importance when the "argument about God" is posed. For that is not a question which, when posed, reveals doubt only in the cognitive or conceptual sense. On the contrary, the question of God is so momentous for the being of the self who raises it sincerely, and so intimately related to the destiny of the self, that the element of detachment which must accompany rational and theoretical formulation will be difficult to achieve. Difficult though it be, however, conceptualization is necessary. On the other hand, religion must always place a high value upon the feeling pole because a religion which does not involve the being of the self is no religion at all. Yet religion must not allow itself to evaporate into mere feeling which is vague and without the guidance of thought. Nor should it be supposed that what is here called the conceptual pole of doubt is "merely theoretical" and therefore to be dismissed as insignificant on the ground that only felt incongruity or uncertainty is genuine or "existential" whereas its theoretical reflection represents "mere rationalism." Both poles are found in all *concrete* religious questioning (i.e. questioning carried on by the sincere and concerned self and not the purely hypothetical sort of inquiry which is to be met with in books of religious apologetic or secular criticism). For if felt uncertainty, the doubt which engages the entire being of the self, is not to remain vague and dumb, locked up within the sphere of feeling, it must be *informed* by an *idea* of the difficulty which spawns it. On the other hand, unless precisely formulated doubt in quest of understanding and rational support is permeated with feeling, with the ultimate concern and participation of the concrete self in the quest, the religious element is lacking and dialectical questioning becomes an empty rationalism or an idle curiosity. The answer to the ancient question whether religious thinking is "practical" (i.e. whether it can legitimately include direct experience and feeling and the demands of practical activity) or whether it is "purely rational" after the fashion of mathematics, must be answered by saying that the antithesis is false because it is based upon a mistaken conception of the sort of doubt and uncertainty which is at the root of all rational reflection in religion. Doubt as it is found in the religious situation has both a felt and a conceptual element in it—an aesthetic-conative aspect and a cognitive aspect. If either is neglected all of the insoluble problems concerning the contrasts between emotive and cognitive, practical and theoretical, will arise.

So important is the phenomenon of doubt for religion and the demand for rational support which it engenders that before proceeding to the question of God's reality it is necessary to consider further the relation between doubt, rational demonstration, and religious faith. As has been pointed out, when we ask for rational proof of the existence or reality * of God, the demand itself shows that the self is in doubt and that such doubt has separated the self from God. Consequently, whatever is able to overcome doubt must also be able to overcome this separation. Although it may be true, as Augustine believed, that God still sustains a relation to the self even in the midst of the deepest doubt, the fact remains that the self uncertain of God is separated from the intimate relation with the religious object which characterizes the life of the man of faith. The self in doubt seeks to remove its uncertainty and to overcome the separation.

The history of Western religion, and of Christianity in particular, shows how frequently the attempt to overcome doubt has taken the form of a quest for rational demonstration or logical proof that the religious object actually exists and, even more, that it *must* be there to be found. The history of the arguments for God, and especially their persistence despite the many times they have been "finally" refuted, testifies to the

* As we shall see, it will not do to identify the two.

power of man's desire to overcome doubt and uncertainty by means of reason. The aim of all the arguments, despite differences in form and content, has ever been the same: to recover the certainty of God's reality and destroy the separation of the self from God which brings doubt in its wake. At this point one of the most perplexing problems in the history of religion presents itself. It may be called the antinomy of demonstration and faith; careful reflection will show that this antinomy has been at the root of most arguments by theologians and philosophers concerning the legitimacy of rational dialectic or proof in matters of religion.

Rational assurance in the form of argument that is rationally compelling involves a measure of distance or separation of the individual self from the object of proof. A living conviction of the truth of faith cannot be established through rational demonstration alone, for the relation between the thinking self and the proposed object of proof is one of theoretical distance, the objectivity of measured form symbolized so vividly by the Greeks in the figure of Apollo. In rational demonstration the logical movement must proceed independently of the heart and will, i.e. the center of the individual self, otherwise the demonstration is not pure and does not fulfill the demands of logical rigor. The self may "accept" a logical conclusion or relate itself to a proposition in a variety of ways, but the validity of the reasoning is not a function of that acceptance or of any of the other relations between the individual self and the resulting conclusion. It is more appropriate to say that the self *acknowledges* a logical conclusion than to say that the self *accepts* it, since a valid conclusion always presents itself as something which a man who recognizes the validity of his rational power at all is compelled to acknowledge; it is not a matter of choice or preference on his part. But it is just the very austerity of this fact which creates a special problem for religious thought; the problem appears with peculiar force when the object of proof is God, the supreme religious object. If the individual self is excluded from participating as an *individual* in the rational process, the self must also fail to participate in or share the conclusion. When the reality of God is made into a necessary logical outcome, to be acknowledged merely as something required by thought, there seems to be room neither for love nor for that voluntary movement toward God which is essential to religious faith. The serious question is this: how is it possible to reconcile the universality and logical compulsion which must accompany demonstration with the individual participation, love, and voluntary turning toward God which characterizes living religious faith? Those who demand that religious faith be rational and thus be capable of existing in the face of critical doubt, and also that it transcend self-indulgence and sentimentality, search for a proof of some sort; for them God must stand as a conclusion toward which we are pushed by thought itself. Whereas, on the other hand, those who are alive to the purely religious values in the situation see that for the individual to stand in the religious relationship there must exist a desire for God and love toward him, both of which seem incompatible with the demand that the self be led to God only as the result of an objective, rational compulsion which is real independently of the individual and his will. This antinomy is unavoidable because there is an element of truth on each side. The demand for *intelligibility*—a demand that Christianity has always recognized in accord with the belief that God is Truth itself—leads us to expect that the reality of God is guaranteed by reason and is thus an objective necessity; on the other hand, the religious relationship is established only when the self desires God and responds in faith, not to a logical conclusion supposed to be universally valid, but to the nature of the religious object itself. The problem of combining a demonstration purporting to be universal with an experience that is intensely personal and individual is a particularly vexing one. In the case of finite objects of proof, the theoretical distance required for objectivity can always be surmounted. With God the problem is more acute. Unless the person acknowledges his involvement in the question of

God, unless he understands that the question is self-reflexive, since it concerns the being of the same person who asks the question, the religious aspect is lost and the question ceases to be a question about God in the full religious sense.

The depth of the antinomy becomes clear when it is understood that the circumstances and conditions of proof in the case of God's reality are such that they seem to endanger the religious relationship by making it a matter of logical constraint rather than a centered act based on faith and love. If the assertion of God's reality cannot survive critical questioning then we must fall into unintelligibility and succumb to doubt, but if demonstration is the only sure means of overcoming doubt and of recovering belief in God we shall have to face the difficulty that in the very act of proving God the self becomes related to God in a manner which distorts the true religious relationship.

There is a solution to the antinomy that threatens to set the demands of thought in irreconcilable opposition to the requirements of faith, and if this solution should prove adequate it will do justice to both of the claims mentioned. There are two main considerations in the solution: one concerns the nature of reason and thought and the other concerns the rôle played by the individual's own experience in the process of tracing out a rational pattern of thought. As regards the nature of reason, we must distinguish between, first, formal reason or reason as purely formal logic or as a system of implications between propositions which rest ultimately upon arbitrarily chosen axioms, and, second, living reason or reason as the quest on the part of the concrete self for intelligibility. In the second sense reason is a living movement of thought related individually to a thinking self; it starts from certain direct experiences and moves toward the discovery of rational pattern and meaning within these experiences. It is an error to suppose that reason in the first sense, important as it is for certain purposes, is the model and archetype of reason itself. Formal reason is better adapted to sciences in which it is not only unnecessary but detrimental to introduce the concerns of the individual thinking self into the situation. Formal reason, however, is inadequate for disciplines more intimately related both to historical events and to the direct, felt experience of selves.

Reason in the sense of living reason needs to be recovered, for it is the form of reason required for all the concrete rational pursuits in which men are engaged—art, morality, politics, and religion. There are several differences between these two ways of regarding reason and rational activity, but for present purposes it is enough to mention but one, namely, the difference over the relation of reason to the individual self that thinks, particularly whether the individual's rational insight into the subject matter is regarded as legitimate, or whether all logical transitions are taken as so strictly a matter of formal rule that no reference to the individual's experience or his relation to the particular subject matter is necessary.

In the formal conception of reason the individual self or reasoner does not figure essentially in the thought process. All logical determination is from beyond his ken, and over against his own direct experience, his individual purpose in life, stands the necessity of purely formal thought. There is no sense in which the self knows or finds itself in its thought, since reason appears as an alien force, moving from proposition to proposition in a timeless continuum, and the concrete self stands related to any of its conclusions only in an external way, i.e. by the accidental connection of compulsion. The rational self, it may be replied, does participate in purely formal reason when it makes an initial decision to accept all conclusions resulting from the use of such reason, but this is only in appearance. The self as concrete individual does not and must not live in its thought; as far as formal logic is concerned there is logical necessity and to that the individual must submit. The individual self is carried along with the movement of formal logic, to the extent to which it is carried along at all, only as an observer viewing the unfolding of necessity; there is no intelligible connection between the concrete individual self, its concern and its destiny in the world, and the conclusions reached by reason in this purely formal sense.

On the other side, living reason is the rational activity of a concrete self and it means the full involvement of that self in the movement of thought. In contrast to purely formal logic, the conception of reason as living, as the carrying out by the self of the purpose of discovering the rational pattern in its own experience, not only involves the individual self but carries that self along with it so that a sense of conviction attaches to the conclusions it has reached. Living reason is not a power alien to the self, a purely universal and abstract set of rules which is indifferent both to the individual thinker and to the differences between various subject matters thought about. Living reason is the process whereby the self seeks to trace out rational pattern in its experiences; the self recognizes and acknowledges its own nature as a rational being in that process. There is no sense of external compulsion and no sense of being determined by a merely formal necessity. On the contrary, when thought is viewed in its actual movement in the experience of the self seeking to understand itself and its world, it carries the self along with it as willing companion; there is no need for thought to force from the self a consent which still leaves the self at heart unconvinced. If reason can be understood not as something alien to selfhood and not as a form which excludes the individual self, but as an essential power of man as the rational animal, many of the objections which have been urged against the relevance of philosophical thought for religion will be overcome.

Exactly how does the direct experience of the individual play a role in a rational process of thought? If the self is to have a sense of conviction concerning the conclusions attained by reason, it must also have a sense of participation in the subject matter being analyzed. Such a sense can be obtained in only one way—through direct experience. If the self is to recognize itself in its thinking and be bound by the outcome of the process of thought, it must also have a sense of participation in the content of thought. This point was discovered long ago by St. Augustine and it has been kept alive within Christianity by the Augustinian tradition. Rational dialectic in religion cannot perform the task it is supposed to perform unless it begins with ideas which themselves have been derived from the direct experience of the individual. Only in this way can the thinking self find itself possessed of genuine conviction for the conclusions attained by its thought.* The more precisely and completely the premises of an argument are divorced from the direct experience of the thinker, the more impossible it becomes for him to find himself genuinely persuaded by the conclusions at which that thought arrives. It is only when the self begins with its own experience, lives in and through it while seeking to trace out the rational pattern implicit in that experience, that the conclusions of thought at once persuade and engage the entire self. Peirce saw this same point when he distinguished between "a proof which needs itself to be experienced" and a proof which "requires experience of the object proved" (3.35). In religion both are necessary, but the former is likely to be ignored and the omission is crucial. Proof in religion has no value unless the individual experiences the rational pattern himself by tracing out that pattern implicit in his own experience.†

To approach religion through living reason and experience is

* This point and further implications have been developed at greater length by W.E. Hocking, *The Meaning of God in Human Experience* (New Haven: Yale University Press, 1912; reissued 1967 with a new Preface by John E. Smith), chap. XXII.

† Kant distinguished between a process of reasoning in which the self is led along by an idea and an argument producing *conviction.* He regarded the teleological argument for God as of the first sort, but maintained that only the moral argument, understood in its practical import, produces conviction. The reason given is suggestive; the moral argument is based on the person's own awareness of himself as a rational being possessing freedom, and it is this participation by the self in the content of the reasoning (a participation which Kant thought lacking in arguments drawn from the concepts of nature) which supplies the conviction. See *Kant's Critique of Judgment,* Trans. J.H. Bernard, 2d Ed., rev. (London: Macmillan & Co.), 1914. App. 91, pp. 418ff.

to return to the Platonic-Augustinian tradition, the tradition which begins with the self and seeks to discover within the experience of the individual an intelligible pattern. The approach is dialectical in the most important of the many senses of that term—it is a *logical dialogue* carried on by the person in reflection upon his own experience. In this regard, dialectic is distinguished from the tradition of purely formal logic stemming from Aristotle, in that the latter places its emphasis on what is objective, universal, external to the individual self and its direct experience. Experience for the Aristotelian tradition is never experience of the individual self; it is always "standard" or "normal" experience, what is common to many men, or what Dewey has called "funded experience." Moreover, the only valid movement of thought recognized is that of logical implication between propositions according to rule. Its ideal is that of objective, formal, compelling proof, not of rational intelligibility for the individual self. It is no accident that through the development of the Western Christian tradition the two dominant philosophical strains within it have remained true to type; the Platonic-Augustinian strain has followed the path of dialogue and contemplation and it has sought for an understanding and intelligibility in religion which requires the direct experience and insight of the individual. The Aristotelian strain, on the contrary, has not begun with the self and its direct experience, but with the world and with objective, precisely formulated knowledge about it.* From such premises it has hoped to pass, by purely logical transitions, to one of its principal goals—the *proof* of the existence of God. And the chief problem of Aristotelian Christianity has always been to connect the individual self, divorced at the outset from direct participation either in the movement of

* Some British philosophers have a vivid and accurate expression describing the sort of proof which formal logicians always desire: these philosophers speak of "knock-down proofs." They represent what has never been demanded by Augustinians and what has always been sought for by Aristotelians.

thought or in its subject matter, with the conclusions reached by the process of thought or argument.* The principal difference between the two approaches is vital for religious thought. The allegiance of the total self is of the essence of religion, hence the thought processes involved in the discussion of religious issues must be such as to engage the self as a whole. Concrete or living reason based upon the self's own direct experiences is such that within it we can no longer describe the self as being "convinced at the top of his head" but "unpersuaded at the bottom of his heart." This sort of opposition persists only if we think of reason solely in the sense of formal logic and the "knock-down" proof. As long as we think of reason in religion only in terms of purely objective, coercive proof, divorced from the individual's own experience and presumably free of infection by human interests and inclinations to such a degree that it presents its conclusions with the force of sheer compulsion, just so long will there be an irreconcilable opposition between rational dialectics and living religious faith. If, however, we no longer think of formal logic and coercive proof as the standard form of reason but can consider instead a living or concrete reason which is rooted in selfhood and experience and seeks more for intelligibility and understanding than for proof, then it will be possible to bring philosophical dialectics into the discussion of religious problems and to help overcome the disastrous split within contemporary thought between the *rational* (which usually means physical science, mathematics, and formal logic) and the *emotive* (which usually means all the most cherished human enterprises —morality, art, religion, and the theory of the state). Intelligibil-

* It is most instructive that in the comprehensive expression of Aristotelian Christianity in the system of Aquinas, direct experience and insight are dismissed in favor of a purely formal conception of reason (natural light), with the result that an authority external to and accidental to the individual self must enter the faith situation to force the will to accept what is not transparent to the self on rational grounds. See the most illuminating article by Tillich on this, "The Two Types of Philosophy of Religion" *Union Seminary Quarterly Review*, I, 4 (May 1946), esp. pp. 6–7.

ity based upon and exhibited within experience is the very essence of rationality in religion; living reason combines rationality and conviction because it lives within individual human experience. Such intelligibility does not purport to be the sort of proof which exists independent of the experience and insight of the individual self. Moreover, the genuinely religious man knows that the demand for a proof which will coerce the self through sheer necessity, quite apart from the self's having to make what Kierkegaard called the "religious movements" or having to take what has been called the "risk of faith,"* is actually the most subtle form of asking for a sign and of trying to achieve the religious relationship in a manner which avoids decision and risk. Those who believe that a man is being self-indulgent when he refuses to wait for "knock-down" proof in religion are mistaken. The man who thinks he has such a proof has God in a manner which coerces him so completely from beyond his will and inclination that he need change nothing in his life nor be affected beyond the scope of his logical acumen. It is the man who comes to God by way of his experience and who becomes convinced through the intelligibility of his experience who has the harder route. He is the one who is more deeply involved as a self, and he not only risks more of himself, but he must pay a greater price if the future proves that he was mistaken.

It is no attack upon the power of reason to deny its identity with purely formal logic and to deny the sufficiency of such logic in the sphere of religion. On the contrary, if it is possible to recover the more contemplative conception of a living reason or quest for intelligibility through dialectic or dialogue, we shall have restored thought to a place of importance in spheres from which it has been forced to retire. When reason is too narrowly conceived those who perceive this narrowness often conclude

* I purposely do not say "leap" of faith. This image is misleading since it implies an abandoning of rational guidance and a sacrifice of form, whereas "risk" expresses the true *adventure* involved and the fact that the faithful self identifies itself with the object of faith.

that if reason is nothing more than formal logic it is better to abandon all attempts at rationality in art, religion, and morality and seek elsewhere for guidance.

Whereas for centuries philosophers and theologians have constructed, criticized, rejected, and defended arguments for the *existence* of God, repeated reference has been made instead to God's *reality*. At an earlier point in the discussion it was stated that the two are not the same. For a variety of reasons it is more accurate to speak of God's reality, and not of his existence. The distinction is not pedantic. Those influenced by discussions about the concept of existence of the sort introduced into philosophy by Kant have raised serious objections to the continued use of this concept in relation to God. In a paper dating probably from just after the turn of the century, Peirce stated the matter very precisely.* He was correct in noticing that, in modern philosophy and in ordinary thought, "to exist" has come to mean "to be part of a system," or, as Peirce put it, "to react with the other like things in the environment." † To describe God as existing in this sense would be to describe him as merely one finite existent besides others *within* a system, and this is precisely where the principal difficulty arises. God has to be understood as the *ground* and *goal* of a cosmic system, the members and parts of which are themselves systems; consequently it is impossible to characterize God as just one more such constituent within any system. Instead of "exist," Peirce preferred to say "real," and it is wise to follow him in this respect.‡ The "real" is what possesses definite characteristics permitting dis-

* See *Collected Papers*, Vol. VI, sec. 495.

† Ibid.

‡ I am accepting the "realism" of Peirce's position at this point without raising or discussing the arguments for or against it in contrast to other alternatives. It is enough to say—and all the more so in respect to God—that the real is what sustains itself apart from the accident of being represented in individual acts of thought. Whether, however, a realism which defines the real as *absolutely* independent of every idea can ever explain the fact of knowledge is another matter which need not be considered here.

tinction and discrimination; it is not the exclusive possession of a single individual and it reveals itself as having a status beyond the self which experiences or thinks it. If "exist" is to continue to have the more restricted meaning just indicated, it becomes nonsense to speak of God's existence, since to do so would mean that God becomes a finite part of a system instead of the ground and goal of all systems.

Tillich emphasized the same point discovered by Peirce, adding a further reason, of considerable theological import, for avoiding the term existence in relation to God. Tillich writes:

> However it is defined, the "existence of God" contradicts the idea of a creative ground of essence and existence. The ground of being cannot be found within the totality of beings. . . . the Scholastics were right when they asserted that in God there is no difference between essence and existence. But they perverted their insight when in spite of this assertion they spoke of the existence of God and tried to argue in favor of it. Actually, they did not mean "existence." They meant the reality, the validity, the truth of the idea of God, an idea which did not carry the connotation of some*thing* or some*one* who might or might not exist.*

If we are to hold, as we must, that in God there can be no intelligible distinction between essence and existence because the two are not disrupted as in finite beings, it becomes difficult to understand how existence can be separated from God and made into a special object of proof. Neglect of this point in the past had led to a discussion of the proofs for God solely in terms of the meaning of "exists," with little or no attention paid to the nature of God.

To avoid confusion, we must speak of the "reality" or the "being" of God rather than of existence. In this way the discussion is not limited in advance by the necessity of having to conceive God as essentially one in nature with the ordinary objects of sense experience. There are many ways and kinds of being:

* Paul Tillich, *Systematic Theology* (Chicago: University of Chicago Press, 1951), Vol. I, p. 205; quoted with the permission of the University of Chicago Press.

triangles and stars, hopes and fears, institutions and civilizations, numbers and implications, all have their distinctive ways of being or ways in which they are "real." Confusion and poverty of thought are the only rewards that come when we insist upon singling out one, and only one, kind of being as if it were the model and standard for every other. The shift from "existence" to "reality" or "being" in discourse about God does not mean, as is sometimes supposed, that critical discussion about whether or not there "is" God becomes impossible. On the contrary, such discussion continues, but on a new foundation. The question is not whether God "exists" as we might argue about the existence of a unicorn or whether there actually is a substance that is both very dense and highly volatile, but whether we are led through experience and interpretation to acknowledge the reality of a unique being possessing that reality in a peculiar way. The most recent discussions of the ontological argument show an understanding of this point in the remark that the reality of God is a question of necessity or impossibility, but not of contingent "existence."

V

The Argument about God

In discussing the argument about God it is important to keep in mind what has been said about the nature and place of doubt in religion, and especially the concept of living reason. Since living reason develops the content of experience actually had by an individual, consideration of the arguments for God from this standpoint will have to be approached in a way somewhat different from the usual. The question of the formal validity of the arguments is by no means the only question to be raised; more important is the discovery of the concrete experience behind them and the sort of intelligibility they lend to experience. The arguments were developed originally under the influence of religious motives and they were intended to have a religious function; the argument about God was never meant to be merely a dialectical exercise. If we are to understand the full import of these arguments we cannot afford to ignore either their religious import or their foundation in experience. If these two aspects are kept in the foreground, the arguments will not be reduced to logical exercises by means of which philosophers express their secularity in refuting the arguments or their piety in defending them.

THE ONTOLOGICAL APPROACH

In order to avoid the confusion stemming from the many different formulations of the ontological argument, it is wise to begin by describing the ontological *approach* to God. The approach is *reflective* in the sense that the individual begins with his own ideas, meanings, experiences, and attempts to develop their implications and consequences. The starting point of the idea of God and what the term "God" means is presumed to be known at the outset. The content of the idea is a peculiar combination of given historical meaning and constructive speculative interpretation. The formula "that than which nothing greater can be conceived" identifies God with the "Absolutely Exalted" or a fullness of Being which cannot be surpassed by any other reality. For the ontological approach, God is understood as the summit of being, of power, of truth, of love. Reflection on the meaning of this idea is to result in one crucial rational apprehension, namely, that if God is correctly expressed in or described by the formula "that than which nothing greater can be conceived," it is necessary that God be real. That is to say, the argument asserts that whoever understands God in this sense will also apprehend that the conception excludes non-existence by rendering it self-contradictory and by removing it from the realm of possibility. More explicitly, the argument asserts that it is not the case that the meaning of the term "God" is grasped while the necessity of existence is not grasped by one and the same reflecting individual. It was for this reason that the one who said "God" and at the same time denied the necessity of existence implied in the meaning of the term he uttered was called "fool" in Anselm's *Proslogium.*

Before proceeding, as is usually done, to a consideration of the formal validity of the argument from a purely logical standpoint, we must understand more clearly the total experiential and religious setting of the reflection that takes place. We can best understand the religious content of Anselm's original argument if we devote attention to his ingenious formula for expressing the meaning of the term "God." The description of God through that formula represents a unique combination of experience and philosophical interpretation. Anselm inherited the record of the continuing experience of God contained in the biblical tradition. He understood the God of Christianity as the God of majesty, of awe-inspiring sublimity, as a God of perfect love and truth who alone is worthy of an absolute loyalty and devotion. Anselm incorporated this conception into his own experience, relived and repossessed it in meditation and reflection; his task was to find a conceptual formula of a philosophical sort that would express the God of an absolute religious devotion. The formula, "that than which nothing greater can be conceived," is the result of Anselm's search.

One who understands the meaning of the term "God" also understands that God is correctly described in the formula. On the one hand, the formula expresses what is meant by God in an historical religious tradition of experience and faith; on the other, it represents an original philosophical interpretation of what it means to be the God of an absolute loyalty and devotion, a reality embodying a Perfection surpassed by no other reality. Anselm synthesized the historically particular with the philosophically universal. He did not speak within and for Christianity alone, and this is why it is wrong to claim that the argument has no significance beyond the limits of Christian revelation. Anselm meant the Christian God indeed, but he identified the God intended through a philosophical formula containing a universal concept of God. There is an identity and there is a difference; comprehension of the ontological approach demands that both sides be taken into account. The identity consists in the fact that the formula means the God of Christian experience; the difference consists in the fact that the God intended is described through concepts inherently universal and not confined to any one religious tradition.

The dual character of the argument that derives from identifying "God" with "that than which nothing greater can be conceived" at once precludes two ways of interpreting the argument that have been advanced on many occasions. We cannot say that Anselm's argument finds it proper locus exclusively within Christian revelation, because the formula upon which the argument rests is philosophically universal. We cannot say that the argument is purely philosophical and independent of every historical religious tradition, because the formula purports to express what is meant by the term "God" in the Christian tradition. Both aspects must be preserved; neither alone expresses the full significance of the ontological approach to God. The question is, how are the two aspects held together? The answer is, *in experience*. Anslem's famous argument represents a reflective excursion aimed at discovering the logical implications of a twofold experience—the funded experience of the tradition in which he stood and his own personal repossession of that experience through reflection on the nature of the supremely worshipful being. What Anselm discovered is that the fund of experience from which his reflection set out is intrinsically intelligible. His argument was more than a logical exercise constructed in order to convince himself of the reality of God; it was rather a reflective dialogue in which he sought for the intelligibility of what he assumed at the outset concerning the nature of God. The intelligibility he discovered was the concept of necessary existence; the consistency of this concept furnished critical support for the faith and experience out of which the concept was developed. Anselm's starting point, taken all by itself, was without critical support; he found such support in the discovery that the supremely worshipful Being cannot be a merely contingent reality, but is either impossible or necessary. On the other hand, Anselm did not divorce the dialectical development of his starting point from its experiential background. He understood that only the two together, experience and the pattern of intelligibility, can lead to the desired result of an experience critically supported. If we take either the experience or the pattern separately we are left with two abstract results: an argument without religious import or an experience without philosophical support.

From the standpoint of logical validity, the principal objection to Anselm's argument has always been that the claim to existence is a peculiar claim and that it requires for its support something more than logical consistency and the direct apprehension of a necessary connection between ideas. In short, it has been objected that existence can be known only in and through experience or encounter, and that it can never be elicited from ideas alone unless those ideas themselves are already the expression of direct experience. The more familiar way of expressing this point is to say, with Kant, that existence is not a predicate. This view is correct if it means that knowledge of the existence of something, or knowledge that things of a certain kind exist, is different from the knowledge involved in knowing that a thing is, for example, blue or large. The argument is that the term "exists" will function differently in propositions than will terms like "blue" and "large," and, if being a predicate is confined to cases like the latter, existence is no predicate. But having said this, we must ask whether the existence of something is such that it has nothing whatever to do with its nature as expressed in predicates like "blue" and "large," since it cannot be denied that we in fact *do* know something about lions, for example, when we know that they exist (i.e. that there are living specimens), even though this information alone would not enable us to say *what* a lion is beyond the reassertion of the fact that there is such a thing.* If this is the case then existence cannot fall totally beyond the range of thought, and yet even when we acknowledge that we do genuinely know something when we know existence we are uneasy about the *establishing* of existence solely upon the basis of an argument and in the absence of the sort of evidence provided when we can exhibit a specimen of the reality in question.

There is a point which has invariably been overlooked in such

* See my article, "Is Existence a Valid Philosophical Concept?," *Journal of Philosophy*, XLVII, 9 (1950) 238–50, reprinted in *Reason and God*.

discussion, and it is this: in the case of familiar objects we do not trouble about *discursive proofs* of their existence, only because we assume that, by getting into their *presence* (i.e. encountering their existence), we know what we mean, and that we can, in principle, always place ourselves at that vantage point where demonstration (ἀπόδειξις) means pointing to the reality itself. Should it be necessary to contend for the existence of a friend at a time when we could not produce him in the flesh, we might seek to argue for his existence from evidence, but even if we did so it would be in the clear knowledge that every hearer would understand exactly what it would be like to be in the presence of that friend; since we have all experienced many people we would all have fairly clear ideas as to the sort of evidence that would point to, if not conclusively establish, the existence of the friend in question. Unfortunately, the case is different with God; part of the problem is that we do not know from ordinary perception what being in the presence of God would be like, and consequently the assurance accompanying our dealings with familiar objects—those that we can "point to" or "exhibit"—fails us and we are led to attempt to show by means of an argument not merely that God exists, but that God *must* exist. And it appears to us that nothing less than this compulsive necessity via the dialectical route will suffice to make up for the vexing fact that in God's case the familiar and seemingly infallible marks of existence are denied to us. The difficulty is most acute at this point; if we are to find God at all we are forced to find God as existing *necessarily*, and yet we have to admit that all we find in our experience are existences that are contingent in nature. We are dubious over the possibility of establishing a *necessary* existence by dialectic alone when we reflect upon the difficulties confronting us even when it comes to proving the existence of something contingent (as in the case of proving the existence of our friend). And if we say that we can support a necessary existent by producing finite existences which *attest to* or *imply* that necessary existence, we are back again where we began, namely, at the point of eliciting existence by an argument in the special case where we cannot be sure that we know what it would be like to be in the presence of the reality in question. This is, of course, another way of saying that no argument for God can take place without an initial idea of God's nature and this in turn can be secured only through direct experience or encounter. Unfortunately, the limitation of our understanding becomes most evident at this point, because this encounter can never have the clarity and obviousness of ordinary perception.

Must we not, therefore, conclude at once that the ontological approach is not valid just because it does propose to reach existence solely on the basis of ideas? Two considerations are relevant to the answering of this question. First, over against the objection that existence cannot be so deduced, it is necessary to cite the fact that the "existence" claimed in this one case of God is peculiar because it is not, and was never intended to be, existence in the sense appropriate to finite beings. That is to say, the existence in question is one which is an existence totally in harmony with essential nature (i.e. God is the only reality who actually possesses himself) in God and such an existence differs from the sort which, as has already been pointed out, characterizes finite beings in a system. Thus it is correct to say, against Kant and others, that the objection to the argument based upon the inappropriate concept of existence is not conclusive. Second, over against this defense there is the difficulty that the conclusion of the argument represents nothing more than the deduction of an existence that is already part of the meaning of the concept of God from which the argument sets out. The question then is, how is this existence known to us? and, even more, what is the justification for the original concept of God? The latter point is essential, because if the conclusion of the argument is to be about God, the basic premise must also be about God; that is to say, the original concept must adequately express the divine nature. In view of these considerations the answer to the question, is the ontological argument valid? cannot be a clear "yes" or "no." The principal objection against it, while clear enough in itself, is not conclusive because of the dual sense of existence involved, and thus we cannot say that the argument is invalid on that ground. This leaves the door to the question of validity open. Nevertheless, the principal objection has a certain force, although it is somewhat different from what has usually been supposed.

The force of the objection is *not* that the necessity of existence does not validly follow from the idea of God proposed, for indeed from a purely logical standpoint which takes account of the special sense of existence involved, the existence, as Anselm rightly saw, does indeed follow. What the classical objection does point out is that the apprehension of necessary existence or the grasping of the conclusion that God must be real *does not provide us with the actual encounter* in experience which is supposed to be required for actual, concrete existence as distinct from the rational apprehension that a God whom we have never *in fact* met must nevertheless be real. The argument provides only *rational encounter* if it is viewed in a purely formal sense; it is as if we knew that there must be at least one person in the universe who loves us without our ever in fact having encountered that person. In view of the novel possibility that the argument might prove necessity in the absence of experiential encounter with the actuality proved, it is imperative to look for the difficulty in another direction. Attention must be directed to where it has rarely been directed in past discussion of the ontological proof, namely, to the meaning with which the reflective self is asked to begin. When we try to consider that meaning we discover that we must go back still further to the experience upon which the original idea of God is based and thus back to the discovery of an original encounter providing the material through which the reflective or living reason moves.

If it is said that the ontological approach begins with the definition of God, the claim may be admitted as long as it is acknowledged that the definition expresses a tradition of belief without which that definition would not exist. Anselm began by presupposing the tradition in which he stood and its belief about the nature of God. Moreover, he had, as the meditative and even prayerful form of expression in his writings shows, his own experience before him, and when he described God as "that than which nothing greater can be conceived," he was summing up not only the traditional belief that God is a fullness of being, of truth, of power and of love, but expressing his own experience at the same time. The fact is that Anselm began not only with a definition of God purporting to be a real definition, i.e. one in which the characteristics in question purport to be essential characteristics, but also with a formulation expressing his own encounter with a reality which may be described as the Absolutely Exalted. It is from this essential formulation of traditional belief and personal encounter that the argument sets out. Thus it is legitimate to hold that the ontological approach begins with a definition of God if it is also remembered what stands behind this definition. It is neither an arbitrary stipulation nor a hypothetical construction, but the expression of a historically conditioned or revealed belief.

The ontological argument should not be considered simply as a logically symbolizable argument to be treated without regard to the concrete meaning of its terms, nor is its validity to be decided merely by answering the question whether "existence" is a predicate like "blue" or "large." The ontological argument must be approached through the experience upon which it is based and it must be taken as the movement of living reason seeking intelligibility within that experience. The reflecting self, participating as a total self in its own thought, starts by considering the meaning of a tradition of experience and belief about the nature of God; the course of the argument represents the path by which the self seeks to develop the implications of the initial point of departure. The central point of the ontological approach is that the reflecting self discovers a fundamental implication following from the meaning entertained at the outset. The person discovers that a reality correctly described as the Absolutely Exalted is a reality of which it is true to say that its non-existence is precluded or, what is the same, that it cannot be taken as no more than a possibility. The rational grasp or apprehension of the crucial logical transition in the argument (namely, the realization that the supposition of non-existence logically contradicts at least one proposition expressing the nature of the Absolutely Exalted) is not itself a matter of direct experience, for no one "directly experiences" the *necessity* of the divine existence; that is a matter for thought alone. What is directly encountered is the Absolutely Exalted itself and what is discovered through reflection is that the God encountered is neither a finite, contingent, nor accidental reality, but one whose existence is necessary. The original encounter forming the empirical ground of the argument provides the self with an initial fact; this fact itself is a sufficient starting point for the religious life. Insofar as the starting point remains in the form of direct experience, however, it is incomplete and in need of reflection; the reflective self acknowledges and seeks to fulfill the demand for intelligibility. The result of reflection is the discovery that the reality initially encountered, when properly understood, implies a *necessary* existence, for in the one case of the Absolutely Exalted the argument is valid. Moreover, support is given to the initial experience because the starting point is now seen to be intelligible. For from that beginning an intelligible consequence has followed and this is possible only if that starting point was itself intelligible.

If the question is raised at this point, does the ontological argument *prove* the existence of God? the answer is both "yes" and "no." The ambiguity need occasion no problem, since it is possible to state precisely in what sense it is one or the other. The argument does not initially prove the existence of God to a self approaching it without understanding the traditional meaning with which it begins and without reflecting on the meaning of the term "God," although even to such a self the logical transition in the argument must present a problem for further consideration. On the other side, the argument does show the self who understands the meaning with which it begins that the reality meant is intelligible and that it possesses its own reality with necessity and not only as a matter of fact or contingently. Interpreting the ontological approach in this way enables us to do justice to both of the central aspects involved, the religious and the rational. For unless the religious meaning is kept in the foreground, the argument in its true purport cannot be understood; it is equally true that if it has no demonstrative force it also provides no intelligibility. The religious aspect is represented in the form of tradition and encounter; the rational element is represented by the one crucial, logical transition. What the rational element achieves is not a "knock-down" proof of the existence of God, carrying the self along with it against its will and experience; the argument instead provides the initial experience with rational support by introducing a twofold intelligibility. First, there is the logical transition *within* the argument itself leading to the conclusion that the Absolutely Exalted is necessarily real (i.e. that unreality in this case is not a real possibility), and second, there is the reflection *about* the argument which reveals the intelligibility of the starting point through the fact that a valid consequence follows from it.* Thus in the ontological approach reason does not provide the first encounter from which the fact of God's reality ultimately derives; experience has the priority because it furnishes the meaning with which the argument begins. But reason does provide rational support because it carries the self along from that starting point to the place where it sees that the reality intended is a necessary reality (i.e. a reality of which the propositional function "x might not have been," when "x" denotes that reality, is always false) and to the further reflection that this rational result makes the initial meaning intelligible.

It may be objected that this reinterpretation makes everything

* No valid consequences can follow from a premise intrinsically unintelligible.

dependent upon the initial encounter of God and that consequently the rational element is wholly secondary in importance. A more explicit way of stating this objection would be to say that the element of rational discovery and compulsion is so sharply hedged in by experience that there is no genuine argumentation taking place. Have we not begun with God at the outset and thus with the very Being whose reality is in question? The direct answer to the latter question is yes, we have begun with God, but that of itself need not invalidate the approach, and for two reasons. First, in *all* concrete arguments, i.e. arguments whose conclusions purport to be true of reality transcending language and logic, there is an experiential pole which can only mean direct encounter, and this in turn means that we have begun by presupposing the reality of the subject matter about which we are to conclude. Second, the religious relationship sets special conditions which we may ignore only at the cost of making rational criticism irrelevant to religion. The most important of these conditions is that the self and its own acknowledged experience must enter essentially into the dialectic; if it does not, the religious relevance of the argument is lost. The relation between the self and God is not a relation which can be imported at the end of the inquiry; this was the whole point about the need for a living reason that leads the individual self through the course of the argument. If the religious element is not present at the outset it will not be present at the end. For these reasons the experiential element must be taken as primary and indispensable.

On the other hand, even in the reinterpreted form of the argument there is to be found a purely logical transition which takes the self beyond the limits of direct experience; the *necessity* of the divine existence is not a matter of encounter * but of

* It is not altogether impossible that we may speak of "rational encounter," and indeed the expression has already been used. But it is done at the risk of confusion, because the results of dialectic are matter of thought and rational apprehension rather than of confrontation in encounter.

rational apprehension. It takes us beyond direct experience without ceasing to be logically related to that experience. Moreover, according to the previous analysis, encounter, while direct, is not immediate and completely devoid of rationality in itself.* This means that it is possible to pass beyond direct experience in the course of developing its meaning and implications in thought without losing an intelligible relation with the experiential starting point.

To return to the objection that the ontological approach is forced to begin with God and thus that it never fully escapes a type of circularity, we must ask whether any other type of approach to God is possible which would remove this difficulty. More precisely, we must ask whether there is an approach to God which does not begin with God but with something else instead. For it has often been supposed that if it is possible to start without God and then proceed by logical steps to the conclusion of God's reality, the charge of circularity will have been removed and the conclusion will be solidly established. This belief and this hope must now be examined by considering the arguments traditionally known as the *cosmological* arguments. In anticipating the results emerging from this examination, we shall find that, while these arguments actually fulfill much less than has been claimed for them by their supporters, the approach itself makes its own unique contribution and thus supplements the ontological way. The question which remains is whether the cosmological approach can be successful apart from the ontological, a question that is related to, but not identical with,

* The only solution to the ancient problem of how experience conceived as originating through encounter with the sensible world can be intelligible and how the objects of intelligibility can be experienced lies in the doctrine of *continuity*. This is suggested by the extreme difficulties raised for Kant's theory of experience by the fact that he made the components of sense and of thought totally different *in kind*. Despite the sound historical reasons for this position it was a doctrine of discontinuity and it is a serious question whether such a doctrine does not preclude the possibility that objects of sense could ever be known by thought.

Kant's well-known claim that all the arguments for God presuppose the ontological argument.

THE COSMOLOGICAL APPROACH

The cosmological approach embraces a variety of traditional arguments; it differs from the ontological approach in that the several arguments do not arise from the attempt to formulate essentially one argument in different ways, but from the attempt to frame several logically distinct arguments. Without distinguishing and developing the several cosmological arguments in detail, we shall indicate the essential nature of the approach to God that is expressed in them. The starting point of the cosmological approach is neither God nor the self, but the world of nature and certain of its features. The essence of the approach is to avoid all explicit beginning with God and to commence instead with empirical reality as present in everyday experience. The aim is to proceed from this point *by way of* the principle of causality (which in this case is not incorrectly described as a principle of sufficient reason) to another fact—the existence of God—which must be admitted if the starting point is admitted. If we consider the classical five ways of Aquinas (and omit from present consideration the fifth way, which has been independently developed as the teleological argument), we shall find that this logical structure is present in all of them. The arguments from change, from efficient causation, from contingent existence, and even the argument from degrees of being,* all ex-

* It is a well-known fact that in discussion of these arguments doubt has been expressed whether the fourth way is not guilty of what Thomists call "ontologism," i.e. whether it is not a covert introduction of the ontological argument and the principle upon which it rests, and thus not true to the cosmological type. Upon the present interpretation it is a cosmological argument because it begins with the world of existing things and then asks for a ground or reason making intelligible a certain feature of those things, namely, the fact that they exhibit differences of degree within a specific kind.

hibit a common pattern: they begin with empirical premises and they conclude that, if the fact asserted in these premises is to be explained, a necessary Being is required. The approach means that we reach God by showing that existing things are dependent for their being and for certain aspects of their natures upon a necessary ground that is beyond any of them.

Although the arguments all begin with the world, it is important to notice that they do not all begin with the world in the same sense. The arguments from change, efficient causation, degrees of being, and teleological or purposefully oriented activity and arrangement single out for attention some specific attribute exhibited in the world or some specific fact which is pervasive and to be found at many levels. The argument from the existence of something (whether it be the cosmos itself or some existent being within the world) which has sometimes been called *the* cosmological argument differs from the others in that it singles out existence itself as the fact with which to begin rather than a particular attribute of that existence. This distinction remains valid even if we admit that it is the *contingency* of existence with which the argument begins and that this is an attribute of existence rather than the fact of existence itself. The truth is that contingency and existence merge; the factuality of existence in the sense in which it figures in the argument is the same as its contingency, and the question from which this argument sets out is the question of how it is possible that what may not exist (i.e. what exists and might not have existed) comes to exist at all. The difference is that, whereas the other arguments seek to find an ultimate reason for certain characteristics exhibited in the world, the argument frequently identified as *the* cosmological argument is more radical and asks for the ground of finite existence as such.

The principal reason for pointing out the difference here is that the argument from existence is not subject to some of the difficulties that beset the others, although they are all subject to a common objection which greatly weakens their religious value.

The major objection leveled against the arguments from change and efficient causation is that they depend upon asserting the unintelligibility (or, what is the same, the impossibility) of a series which has no first term; the contention is that this assertion is unwarranted. Russell, for example, has argued that the existence of mathematical series which have neither first nor last terms furnishes us with an illustration to the contrary and that consequently we cannot allow the contention that every series must have a first term. This objection is very far from being conclusive in view of the fact that the series in question are *not* series whose members are empirical *events* (even if they are validly said to correlate with such series), but mathematical entities. Apart from a special argument showing that the particular series referred to in the arguments for God are of the type that need have no first term, the objection easily fails to be conclusive. On the other hand, it must be admitted that in the arguments from change and efficient causation much depends upon the fact that for as many terms (moving from moved to mover and from effect to cause) as we care to take each will itself require a predecessor and thus each one accessible to us will fail to be the *first* term required.* The desired conclusion of a necessary first term depends upon the general consideration that the regress can be stopped at a point only if there is a term requiring no predecessor, i.e. a term which is self-moving or self-caused. And it is here that a *general* appeal to intelligibility becomes necessary; the First Cause and the Prime Mover can be reached only by invoking the principle that the entire series is unintelligible (in this case "unintelligible" means "would not be possible and is actual only as a brute or unexplained fact") unless there is a first term. The argument, then, takes the form that there *must* be a first term if there are any terms at all, and this term will differ significantly from every other since the function performed by the predecessor of any term in the series will have to be performed

* *Immanuel Kant's Critique of Pure Reason*, Trans. Norman Kemp Smith (London: Macmillan & Co., 1933), B537.

for this term by the term itself. The questions presenting themselves are, to what extent is the argument dependent upon the general consideration that intelligibility requires an end to the regress? and to what extent do we actually grasp the necessity of the first term through the facts of change and causation?*

Kant saw that the necessity involved is a necessity of thought or intelligibility, since we do not have the same direct access to the necessary term that we have to all the other terms in the series. It was this consideration that led Kant to claim that the cosmological arguments are dependent upon the ontological—the conclusion of these arguments, he contended, are all necessary thoughts, and the transition from these thoughts to the realities they intend can be made only via the ontological argument. Kant's contention should be amended to read: the cosmological arguments depend not upon the ontological argument as such, but upon the basic principle implicit in the ontological approach, namely, that *a necessity of thought determines a corresponding reality*. This should not be taken to mean that the cosmological arguments are identical in form with the ontological, for they are not, but it does call attention to their dependence upon the general demand for intelligibility and the further principle that whatever is demanded by thought for explaining a fact is itself to be counted among the real.

The objections that have in the past been urged against the cosmological arguments that begin with some particular fact about the world do not enter if we consider the argument from contingent existence, often taken by philosophers (for example, Leibniz and Descartes) as *the* cosmological argument. This form of the argument is more elemental than any other because it does not direct attention to any specific feature of the world,

* The point here is that the more the argument is made to depend upon the general principle of intelligibility rather than upon special insight into the particular facts upon which the argument sets out, the more difficult it becomes to deny the force of an objection like Russell's simply on the ground that it is a general argument and thus unconnected with the particular series in question.

but raises instead the question of the *existence* of finite entities. This argument undercuts the others because it touches the reason for existence of finite things rather than some particular fact about these things. It starts with the assertion, "something exists," and claims that the existent taken both *individually* (proper or finite parts of the cosmos) and *collectively* (the cosmos as a system possessing a grade of togetherness sufficient for it to be taken as one system) is something of which we can say, "it might not have existed." From an examination either of what does exist distributively or of its togetherness as a system, we cannot conclude with confidence that the something in question exists of necessity. Failure to discover *within the nature of the existent* any reason warranting its necessity reveals the contingency of that existent or, what is the same, the fact that it might not have existed. What in fact exists and might not have existed does not bear the reason or ground of its existence within itself but in another. The argument may then be stated as follows: if anything exists and everything might not have existed, which is in fact the case for the finite existents accessible to us, then there must be at least one existent capable of giving existence to itself, or, which is the same, one existent which necessarily exists. What this argument reveals in a more radical and devastating way than the others is the fact that finite or contingent existence is not self-supporting—God as the necessary existent is not identical with the world or with any of its proper parts.

This line of argument is valid in itself, but it must be noticed that it depends upon the general demand for intelligibility for its success. Should it be objected that the regress from contingent existent to contingent existent need not logically be stopped, or that if it is stopped somewhere the term chosen will still be a contingent, finite existent, the only reply possible is that total *intelligibility* demands a necessary existent, otherwise the contingent existences remain unexplained. If we stopped the regress at a finite existent, intelligibility would not be attained. Invocation of the principle of intelligibility or sufficient reason is the only way of stopping the regress; if the principle is disallowed the cosmological argument fails.

What does this result mean and how are we to interpret the principle leading to it? It means that contingent existence individually and the world as a system do not contain within themselves the ground of their own existence; this ground, if found at all, will have to be beyond them. That there is in fact such a ground can be determined from the reflective standpoint only if reality exhibits the intelligibility which is called for in the principle of sufficient reason. This point may be expressed in another and quite surprising way by saying that such complete intelligibility is what we would expect reality to exhibit *if God were real.* The principle itself, namely, that there is an ultimate intelligibility both for the features exhibited in the world and for the existence of the world itself, *is a way of expressing what it would be for God to be real.* If this surprising result correctly represents the case, the question at once arises, have we not argued in a circle? Is it not the case that these arguments lead to the conclusion of a first cause, a necessary existent, etc., only by the invocation of a principle which expresses part at least of what is meant by saying that God is real? This is in fact the case; the cosmological arguments are actually arguments from God to God and not solely from the world to God as they appear to be. But it should not be concluded that the arguments are simply void and useless; the cosmological approach makes an unique contribution in that the arguments, and particularly the argument from the fact of existence itself, make explicit the insufficiency of finite existence. They demonstrate its incompleteness and testify to the fact that finite existence, as it stands, is neither self-explanatory nor self-supporting. This fact is not a logical consequence of the principle of sufficient reason, but is discovered to be true of finite existence when that principle is invoked. Moreover, since what is shown to be without rational support when taken by itself has the nature of a fact, there is a strong presumption that the reality supporting it and making it intelligible must have the status of fact. Finite existence is not explained and supported by what has no more than notional or hypothetical status. This is a contribution of great importance and it is probably what was meant by those thinkers who urged the superiority of the cosmological approach over the ontological. The ontological approach has not ordinarily been taken as beginning with a matter of natural fact, whereas the cosmological arguments do take their rise from such fact and suggest that God is related to it, is expressed in it, and forms the ground of its existence. The ontological approach, by contrast, makes no clear reference to the relation of the divine to the cosmos.

The cosmological approach, it will be recalled, was to start not with God but with something else, and then to argue toward God so that God would appear only at the end and not at the beginning. A serious problem confronting this approach, however, is that of connecting the necessary existent reached via the various cosmological routes with God as understood in the religious tradition within which the thinker exists and believes.* This problem has long been recognized, but it has not been taken with sufficient seriousness by theologians and religious thinkers. Thomas Aquinas, for example, passed over it too rapidly, and, after having arrived at the conclusion of a Prime Mover, a First Cause, etc., he went on to identify these realities with the God of Christianity simply by saying, "and this every-

* If it is said that a thinker not claiming to represent an identifiable or classical religious tradition does not have this problem on his hands, the reply is that he then must claim to be defining God *de novo* and the conclusions of his thought must remain logically unrelated to the concept of God as understood from the standpoint of the religion he eschews. In the past no end of confusion has been generated by philosophers who began by denying all influence from or concern for the dominant religious tradition of the culture in which they existed, but who have then gone on to assume that what they say about God is somehow representative of or relevant to the religious beliefs of which they have claimed to be independent. We must repeat a principle previously expressed: a thinker is always at liberty to mean what he pleases, but he is not at liberty to claim that what he pleases coincides with what other people actually mean when they express their beliefs.

one understands to be God" or "to which everyone gives the name God," etc. And it is clear that, as a Christian theologian, he must mean by God the one understood to be God in the Christian tradition. It is true that his position does not require him to hold that God is *fully known* by inference from the world and its features, because this approach gives us no more than God as he is to us and through another and thus not in himself. On the other hand, there must be a *point of identity* between the God known through the cosmological arguments and the God known through the Christian tradition. This identity cannot be secured unless there is an essential connection between the reality reached via the cosmological route and the God understood to be God at the beginning of the argument. Granting that the connection is required, if the arguments are to be religiously relevant the problem presenting itself is this: how shall we maintain with confidence that the reality elicited from the contingency of the world (and thus from general or publicly accessible experience formulated in empirical premises) is in fact identical at least in part with the reality called God as understood by Christians? In order to answer this question it is necessary to go behind the cosmological approach and ask whether a concept of the reality that is to be reached through the arguments is present among the unexpressed premises of the reasoning. Should this prove to be the case, a new light would be thrown upon the traditional view that the ontological approach starts with the idea or definition of God whereas the cosmological way begins with the world and reaches God only at the end of the argument. It may be that the idea of God is introduced at the outset in the cosmological arguments and that it is only by virtue of this fact that the connection between the God of the religious tradition and the necessary existent of the arguments can be established.

The question naturally arises whether the connection between the Prime Mover, the First Cause, etc., and God is external or whether some intelligible connection is to be found. Further consideration of this question points to a dilemma. If the specifically religious conception of God is presupposed at the outset it cannot be said to result from the arguments themselves, and in that case the connection between the terms in question would seem to be gratuitously assumed. But if there is no connection between God and the Prime Mover, the necessary existent, etc., it would follow that God does not appear or make himself known through the world of finite things. This is a consequence which the Judeo-Christian tradition cannot accept in view of the strong emphasis placed on God as creator and as one who manifests himself in nature. Unless the cosmological arguments are to be dismissed as *religiously* unimportant, the connection between the religious conception of God and the necessary Being of the arguments must be discovered. The connection can be established only if the cosmological arguments explicitly begin with an idea of God embracing the functions and characteristics of the divine nature which are revealed in the cosmos and are made known through the arguments. There is no way of connecting God with the Being reached through the arguments unless the connection is presupposed at the outset. The cosmological arguments must therefore begin with the initial assumptions that God is, first, actually manifested in the world, and, second, is inclusive of the functions and characteristics discovered via the cosmological route.

The fact that such a problem arises shows that God is not completely manifested in the cosmos and that each of the arguments presents us with but an aspect of the divine nature; no one selected aspect of the world is sufficiently rich to reveal or express the full being of God. God as Prime Mover, for example, does not exhaust God, since God also redeems and sustains, and neither of these aspects of God follows from the idea of a source of motion and change in the world. At this point the most important limitation of the cosmological approach becomes evident; insofar as it is confined to the created world and to certain of its features to the exclusion of man and his inner experience of himself, the cosmological approach reaches God only as

He is known through the public and repeatable features of the cosmos. The historical particularity of distinctly human experience and the conception of God distilled from such experience (the God known, for example, through and in the life of Moses, Jesus, and Paul) will not be uniquely derivable from the cosmological starting point because that experience does not follow from the cosmological premises. And yet if the cosmological way is to retain its religious meaning it is essential that the god to which it can attain is identical with God manifested in historical religious experience. Failure to establish the connection leaves the religious conception without cosmological fulfillment on the one hand or it deprives the cosmological approach of its religious significance on the other.*

The problem nevertheless remains of discovering how the needed identification between the necessary Being of the cosmological arguments and God is to be maintained in a fashion which is intelligible. There is but one way in which this can be done, namely by *assuming at the outset* (this is the element of existential commitment in the cosmological approach) *that God is already known to have a nature of a certain sort and that this nature includes the power of being expressible in the world.*

* It is evident that behind the discussion stands the ancient distinction between *natural* and *revealed* theology and religion. Much confusion could be avoided if the basic motive behind the distinction were given a different form of expression. The distinction intended is actually a difference in the medium through which God is known; natural theology finds God in the public and repeatable aspects of the cosmic process—what Whitehead has called "general occasions." Whereas revealed theology makes normative the crucial historical events and personages of a historical community—what Whitehead has called "special occasions." The difference is real and undeniable, but it poses the enormous problem of discovering how the two types of occasions are related to each other. The historical particularity is not derivable from the general occasions, which is precisely why the eighteenth century, for example, could attain to the supreme Being in their natural religion, but not to the God attested to by Moses and Jesus. On the other hand, unless it is assumed that the God of historical religion is able to be known through the cosmos there is no possibility of establishing intelligible relations between the two types of occasions.

This means that the specific cosmological type arguments all assume some one aspect of God, such as that of First Cause, or Final Cause, which correlates with the cosmological aspect selected. In this regard, it is more accurate to say that the arguments yield necessary functions of God in relation to the world rather than God himself, God being presupposed at the outset as capable of expressing himself in the cosmological features.

The fact that the arguments rest on an initial assumption does not destroy their value, since their primary function is to provide further determination of the necessary reality which the arguments yield. Without that initial assumption, however, the cosmological arguments must remain unconnected with God as conceived by a historical religious tradition.* And this is precisely why theologians of the later Middle Ages moving toward God via the cosmological approach were constantly embarrassed; their arguments were markedly similar, but the conceptions of God current in their historical religious traditions were different and there seemed to be no warrant for identifying the necessary Being at which they arrived with the God who spoke to Moses, or was in Christ, or who was proclaimed by Mohammed. The reason for the difficulty is clear; the cosmological starting point is not sufficient in its religious depth to enable the mind to move from it to the full religious conception of God. When the deficiency is removed by making the assumption previously indicated; the cosmological approach, *like the ontological in this respect*, can no longer be said to set out from the world alone, but must be seen as beginning with God. This fact may not be noticed, since attention is directed primarily to the world, but the conception of God is presupposed and its presence is revealed with dramatic swiftness when it is held, as it

* From a speculative standpoint we can say that, armed with a full and perfect knowledge of the world, we could trace out the nature of the divinity by working from the world back to God. But even as a speculative program this would be possible only if we knew that God were fully *manifested in the cosmos* or in the nature of those finite realities from which the arguments take their start.

must be, that the First Cause or Prime Mover is in fact that God of the Christian or Islamic traditions. From the religious standpoint the cosmological approach cannot stand alone; it requires for completion a starting point which is the same as that of the ontological approach, and in this sense the one is not independent of the other.*

THE TELEOLOGICAL APPROACH

As has aleady been suggested, the teleological approach properly belongs to the category of cosmological arguments, since, like them, it proposes to approach God by starting with the world of nature. And insofar as it is a cosmological type of argument, what has been said about that way of approach will hold for the teleological argument as well. The teleological way has, however, at least two features which serve to distinguish it from its near neighbors: first, it seems closer to ordinary experience and observation than the other "more philosophical" proofs, and second, in viewing the world in its totality as the expression of a self-conscious plan the argument more closely approaches the idea of God as a purposive Being (and thus as a *self*) than is the case with the other cosmological proofs. As regards the first point, it is a well-known fact that the abundance of orderly process in the world has impressed the mind of man from the beginning of recorded history. The theme is one of universal recurrence in all religious literature, and when the Psalmist asked, "He that made the eye, shall he not see?" (Psalm 94:9), he was

* The dependence here mentioned, namely, the dependence involved in the fact that the cosmological arguments all require beginning with a concept of God, is not to be confused with the other sense in which these arguments have been said to imply the ontological approach. The latter relationship is best clarified by saying *not* that the one set of arguments presupposes the ontological argument, but that the *ontological principle* (namely, that a necessary idea is determinative of reality) invoked in the ontological argument is also required if we are to make the transition from the necessary ideas to the reality correspondent.

expressing what had so often been noted and asked by thinking men. The accessibility of nature made it inevitable that man should seek in its order and pattern some clue to its origin and to his own destiny. Moreover, the argument from design expresses a quest for a *purposive* power in the universe capable of accounting for the order and adaptation to function displayed in it. The argument reaches out for or points to a self-conscious Being insofar as the idea of *deliberate plan* has figured in the many formulations of the proof. Unless the element of purposiveness (or "design" in the sense in which we say that a deliberate act was done "by design" or "on purpose") is involved there is no need for introducing a self-conscious Being. The fact of order taken quite apart from the supposition that it is chosen purposely so as to achieve some ultimate purpose for the world might be explained by other means. A merely immanent order might belong to a system necessarily and not contingently and hence would require no reference to a source beyond itself. It is therefore essential to the teleological approach that the order itself be seen as requiring explanation and thus as contingent in the same sense as the other cosmological characteristics.

From a logical standpoint, the design argument has a peculiar form. As expressed by many thinkers of the past it assumes the form of a four-termed analogy in which three terms are believed to be known through ordinary experience, with God as the required but not directly presented missing term. So taken, the argument would mean that, just as a mechanic or watchmaker is needed to explain the existence of a complex and smoothly functioning mechanism or system containing parts the natures of which are uniquely derivable from their actual function in that system, the system of adapted parts which is the world requires a mechanic or architect for its explanation. The ground for the transition from the effect to the cause would not, however, be the same on both sides of the equation. It would not be by means of any "sheer" deduction that we arrive at the existence of the finite watchmaker, since the reason for inferring his existence is that we have made instruments of this kind and find *in our experience* no case where such an adapted mechanism "just comes to be" without a watchmaker. On the other side of the equation, however, we have no such guide, since not only does the total system of nature differ fundamentally from the corresponding finite mechanism, but the world is not one member besides others of a class of phenomena from which inductions might be made; there may be many watches but there is only one world of nature. Once again the general sort of difficulty so much emphasized by Kant presents itself—we are never in a position to grasp a system like nature as a whole in the sense in which we can encompass one of its proper parts. And in virtue of this fact the four-termed syllogism will not only require the discovery of the fourth term for its completion, but will stand in need of supplementation in the form of further knowledge of the third term—the world—as well.

Curiously enough, however, virtually all criticisms of the design argument have been directed against its concrete content and not against the analogical form it has assumed. Even so skeptical a critic as Hume was not ready to maintain that the analogical argument proved nothing at all.* What he did maintain—and Kant at times followed the same line—is that the facts of design and adaptation in the basic premises do not permit us to conclude that there is an "all-powerful," "all-wise," or "creator" God. Kant's two principal objections to the argument (which, incidentally, he treats with greater respect and circumspection than the others, see *Critique* B 652) were first, that it points to a designer fashioning already existent material according to a plan, but not to a creator in the classical sense, and second, that we cannot know from the cosmos as such that its architect is "all-wise" or "all-powerful," since we have no standard of comparison that enables us to arrive at this judgment. The most we can say on Kant's view is that the designer has just the power and the wisdom to fashion what in fact presents itself to us.

* It is instructive that whereas many thinkers have flatly claimed the ontological and cosmological arguments to be logically false, no one has claimed to be able to remove *all* logical force from the design argument.

The important point in Kant's criticism is that it directs attention to the concept of God and, instead of denying all force to the logical structure of the analogy, it is aimed instead at exposing the gap between what the cosmological premises can yield and the God of the religious tradition.* Kant saw that even if nature or the cosmos were taken as thoroughly organic in character (rather than as mechanical) and thus as requiring something more than a non-self-conscious artificer to explain it, theoretical reason confronted with such a nature could still not derive from it that divine reality necessary from the religious standpoint. Kant saw that it was necessary to go beyond the theoretical consideration of the cosmos, or, what is the same, to attend instead to the experience of what is *specifically human*—expressed by him as the practical employment of reason—in order to obtain a starting point for a sound theology. This development serves to point up in another way the necessity of starting with the conception of God required by the religious consciousness and the manifest impossibility of arriving at that conception merely from the consideration of the world or of any experience which excludes what is specifically human. The fact is that the God to be arrived at *through the cosmos alone* must always be limited to those features of the world selected and to their inherent capacity for bearing or expressing the divine nature. Our acquaintance with our fellows, for example, is strictly conditioned by the capacity of the relations or contexts in which we meet them to reveal the nature of their selves, and we shall not attain profound insight into another self if that self is revealed to us only under the most trivial circumstances. The situation is not different with respect to God; the God we can arrive at will depend upon the revelatory capacity of the medium selected. The chief difficulty with the cosmological approach, important as it is for preserving the expression of God through the natural world, is that it must ignore the specifically human experiences from which the religious conception of God ulti-

* See *Kant's Critique of Judgment*, sec. 85.

mately derives. No cosmological type of argument, confined to nature and its features, can reach the concept of a self-conscious purpose which is of the essence of the religious conception of God. Another way of expressing this is to say that the cosmos, considered solely as the object of theoretical knowledge, cannot lead the self to the idea of the good which is essential for the concept of purpose. It is for this reason that arguments of the cosmological type, when employed in the religious context, are all dependent upon an initial conception of God assumed at the outset and not derived from the analysis of nature or the form of the argument itself.

The cosmological approach can be of value only to the extent to which its two-fold deficiency is understood. First, it requires the introduction of the ontological principle and is thus not self-contained, and second, it depends upon a conception of God which it cannot furnish from its own resources. Kant saw both deficiencies and his acute awareness of the second led him to the moral sphere, the sphere of specifically human experience, as providing the only proper starting point for theological reflection. If, from the standpoint of human experience, we consider the two classical starting points of all religion and theology—the cosmos and man—man is the more fundamental, for, among other reasons, man is the only religious animal.*

THE ANTHROPOLOGICAL APPROACH

In seeking to approach God through specifically human experience it is necessary to revive the pattern of thought and experi-

* The Augustinian tradition has always insisted upon this point. See, for example, Bonaventura's *The Mind's Road to God*, for a distinction between the *traces* of God and the *image* of God; both are expressive of the divine presence, but the former are found in nature and are less adequate than the latter which is found in man alone. Notice, that it is incorrect to speak of *images* in the plural, since it is man as such who both *is* and *has* the image; *traces* are, on the other hand, legitimately plural since they are found throughout nature.

ence out of which the ontological approach first arose. It is necessary to return to the way of Augustine and the Platonic tradition; the self must retire into itself, for the conception of God is first realized in this self-reflective encounter. As was maintained in the discussion of the ontological argument, the starting point for each individual is a combination of an idea inherited from a classical religious tradition and a direct encounter in experience of a reflective sort. In such reflection one discovers, to use the expression employed before, that the Absolutely Exalted has been present *at some point* in his experience. In maintaining that the encounter with God is direct but not immediate, the aim is to provide for the fact that all initial encounter with God is mediated, in the precise sense that there is *no experience of God that is not at the same time experience of something else*. That is to say, the presence of God is always mediated by signs or comes through a medium, even though the presence itself is genuine and the experience direct. Since "no man hath seen God at any time," it becomes essential for man to know what experience or trait of experience is to be taken as the sign of the divine presence. The need for such a clue (which cannot possibly be derived from further experience without vicious circularity) * marks the limit of pure empiricism in religion and of all purely "natural" theology. The indication or sign of the divine presence is supplied by or found implicit in the inherited religious tradition.

Following the path marked out by the Augustinian tradition, we may ask: where in reflection upon our experience can we find the presence of the Absolutely Exalted? There are three fundamental points at which this reality may be experienced, or three marks of the presence of the divine. One represents the experience which Kant found decisive for his so-called "moral argument," although there is no need to confine the religious dimension unduly by restricting it to the moral alone.† We may

* Royce's "paradox of revelation" is relevant at this point.

† In referring to the present approach as "anthropological" instead of as the "moral approach" the aim was to make it possible to include the whole range of experience relevant and not only the experience of obligation.

express the same point by saying that there are other dimensions of experience in addition to the moral where the presence of the Absolutely Exalted is to be detected. The three together are to be taken as expressing in further detail the concern for our ultimate destiny singled out as the basis upon which religion itself might be characterized or defined in its essential nature.

The three signs or marks of the presence of the divine are the three points at which the self and its experience are touched by an unconditional element containing a *question* and a *concern* and thus combining both a conceptual and a feeling pole. These three points in experience involve questions to the extent to which we are aware of quest for meaning, and they involve concern to the extent to which one making the quest is aware that the answer is internally related to his own being and to the quality of his life and thus is not a theoretical quest in which he may or may not be involved. The three occasions are: the awareness of the contingent character of one's existence and the question of, and concern for, the ground or the *from whence* of life; the awareness of the limit of existence in non-existence or death and the question of, and concern for, the goal or ultimate destiny of life, the *to whence* of life; and the awareness of being a responsible being and the question of, and concern for, the moral direction and quality of the self in its concrete, historical existence. When man encounters these three points at which his life is related to something unconditional, he encounters the signs or marks of God. The Absolutely Exalted is present in these experiences and the task of rational reflection is the recovery of that presence through the discovery that those marks are indeed the genuine marks of God.

It must not be thought that the anthropological approach to God merely offers a new datum from which to infer the existence of God. There is a vast difference between starting with a datum from which to infer the existence of something else and starting with an experience which contains in itself the presence of a reality not immediately known as such. In the first case we start with what purports to be a fact open to all, an objective datum that is to serve as a premise for an argument to something beyond it. In the second case we have a concrete self existing within an experience and aware of the internal connection between that experience and its own being; here the self does not take the experience as a datum initiating a process of inference, but as a portion of its life within which it dwells while it seeks to understand that experience and permeate it with reflection. In the first case the objective datum is left standing outside the process of reflection and is in fact lost as an experience for the thinking self just because the self withdraws itself from it, and views it merely as an objective fact from which to argue. In the other case the self dwells within its experience and seeks its intelligibility, an aim quite different from that of using the experience as a datum from which to infer the existence of something else. We may say that finding God present through reflective understanding of experience is not the same as arguing from that experience to the existence of a God never understood as being present. The difference between arguing from a datum and developing the meaning of an experience is decisive for the whole of the philosophy of religion.

But, we may ask, what is the nature of the reflection that moves within the experience and remains related to the concrete individual self that reflects? How does it differ from the situation in which experience is objectified, divested of its relation to the one who has it, and transformed into a piece of evidence from which the existence of something else is to be inferred? To say that experience is objectified means that some particular experience, such as seeing green or feeling sad, is taken as a settled fact to be observed or explained by *any* self fulfilling the conditions for attaining valid knowledge. The contrasting situation differs from this in two respects: *first,* the reflecting self is reflecting upon its own experience as something had and lived through (that is, there is a self-reflexive factor present and acknowledged) and *second,* the reflecting self does not seek to *observe* the object of its reflection in order to explain it or discover its causes; it seeks instead to *understand* experience, to discover the bearing of any particular item or aspect of experience upon the total pattern or purpose of its own self. When experience is objectified (as it must be for purposes of theoretical investigation) its peculiar relation to the life and destiny of the individual self who has it must be ignored; objectified experience must be treated as *anybody's* experience and appropriately taken as evidence available to all. For objectified experience, the bearing of that experience upon the life pattern or plan of an individual self does not count, and yet that bearing is just what is essential from the religious standpoint. We must conclude that the reflection or reason that functions in religion does not follow the pattern of arguing from objective evidence to the existence of something else never encountered; on the contrary, if we would understand reason in religion we must see it as a quest for intelligibility where the reflecting self moves through its own experience and seeks to apprehend its full content and bearing. The discovery that God can intelligibly be believed to have been present in an experience we have had but that we did not at the time know it to be an experience of God is vastly different from the situation in which we argue from a settled fact that God must exist, or conclude that another existent can be deduced from a given datum although we ourselves have had no experiential connection with the conclusion and have in no sense encountered the reality proved.

It may be asked whether there is a genuine logical transition present in a reflection of this sort. The answer to this question is yes, but the nature of the transition differs from that of deduction. Reflection within experience leads to the discovery that a reality already encountered manifests the presence of something else not immediately known as such at the time; reflection is not properly to be taken as inference from something experienced to something else that is then proved to exist. In the experiences described as the points at which the unconditional element is present, one must see in them the signs which reveal the presence of

God. The process whereby religious experience becomes intelligible is not one of formal demonstration, but rather one of *interpretation* in which certain signs apprehended stand in need of being read or interpreted. When interpreted, these signs are understood as the medium through which the divine presence is revealed. The rational movement is from experience through the signs to the discovery that in the very experience with which we have begun there is present a reality not known as such at the time of initial encounter. If we could know this presence immediately there would be no need for the rational process, but since there is no experience of God which is not also the experience of something else at the same time, it is necessary to move through the signs, interpret them, and thereby arrive at the conclusion that in having those initial experiences we were actually in the presence of God.

At this point we are in a position to point out a third way in which reflection differs from purely formal reasoning: in reflection the movement from the initial experience to its interpretation is not a movement away from the starting point to something else, but rather the discovery that there is more actually present in the starting point than we knew. The discovery of a reality present in a starting point is different from arguing that a given starting point used as a premise requires the existence of something beyond but not present in it.

In the light of the foregoing, arguments for the reality of God take on a new meaning. Instead of being viewed as a syllogistic process of passing from a datum to the necessary existence of another datum, they become processes of interpretation whereby experience is made *intelligible* and its full content is made explicit. That is to say, what is present in experience, though not immediately apprehended as such, becomes clear and explicit through interpretation and understanding. This was precisely the original intent of the formula "faith seeking understanding," except that the religious starting point need not be "faith" in the sense of authoritatively received propositions, but rather certain experiences that are to be taken as signs. The interpretation of these signs, to be sure, will not be possible apart from the guidance of leading ideas derived from an historical religious tradition, but the authority of that tradition will not be assumed at the outset as it was in the ancient formula. Too often Augustine and even Anselm wrote as though their starting point ("faith") represented a certainty that is self-enclosed and sufficient so that consequent understanding is only a superfluous addition. Such a view nullifies the critical or rational element. A more defensible view holds that the intelligible development of experience makes an indispensable contribution, and that *the very intelligibility itself* is a factor, and indeed the most important factor, in bringing the self to accept and commit itself to the reality of the divine presence.* Unless this rational function is taken seriously, understanding can be no more than a superfluous addition to a previously assumed certainty. The reason that Kierkegaard could complain about those for whom a "simple" faith is not enough, and about those who pretend to "understand" faith in a sense more profound than is possible for bakers and tailors, is that his initial faith standpoint is taken to be certain or self-contained; it neither needs nor can it attain to any support or supplement. The result is that intelligibility is deprived of its power in the religious situation; † interpretation and rational understanding are denied a role in *determining* commitment. This consequence is especially to be deplored because it sets up an irreconcilable opposition between religion and reflection and widens the gap between philosophy and theology; the result is that theology be-

* Here we must distinguish between faith in God making human existence intelligible and the making of the experience of God intelligible. The experience of God does not become intelligible merely because the presence of God makes human existence intelligible.

† There is a curious inconsistency at present in the works of theologians who, on the one hand, reject philosophical mediation in theology, but who then go on to argue that a religious view is validated because it alone "makes sense" out of life as no other view does. This "making sense" is precisely the appeal to intelligibility.

comes more dogmatic and undialectical (i.e. uncritical) and philosophy becomes more insensitive to the religious issues.

We may attempt to summarize the main points of the extended discussion concerning the argument about God. First, it is essential to return to the ontological approach to God with the reflective self as the starting point. From this standpoint God can be a matter of encounter, in contrast with the cosmological approach which requires that we argue from a finite reality to a necessary existent that is never encountered. The ontological approach must be taken in conjunction with the anthropological approach, since man is the only being in which there comes to consciousness the question of, and concern for, the meaning of being, or the unconditioned ground of existence. The approach to God through the unconditioned points in experience is not to be taken as a case of arguing from this experience back to the existence of God. Taken in that sense, the anthropological approach is converted into a cosmological one with man's "experiences" supplying the empirical data for the argument. But this is to objectify experience and to transform it into a datum to be observed rather than something to be lived through and understood by the self who experiences. Instead of using his experience as a means of proving the existence of God, each individual must attempt to recover in *his own* experience the *presence* of the divine in the crucial experiences.

The ontological approach taken in conjunction with the anthropological approach leads us to ask these questions: At what points in experience is the divine presence to be detected? Where is the Absolutely Exalted as the supreme object of worship and devotion to be encountered? What experience must be developed reflectively in order to discover that presence which is the divine? There are three points in human experience at which the self, retiring into itself and inquiring, encounters the divine through signs. First, in the awareness of the contingent and derivative character of human life involving the question of, and concern for, the *from whence* or ground of life; second, in the awareness of the limit of human life and the anticipation of death involving the question of, and concern for, the ultimate destiny of the self; third, in the awareness of freedom and responsible action involving the question of, and concern for, the ground and content of obligation or the direction which human life *ought* to take. At these points, points where human existence touches its own ground, the reality of the divine is encountered. The Absolutely Exalted is grasped by the reflecting self able to understand its own experience; only through understanding and interpreting can the self discover in these signs the presence of a reality whose nature it is to be present and directly experienced, but not immediately known.

VI

Experience, Community, and the World Religions

Religion is nothing if it is not established in the individual person, but it is equally lacking in substance if it is confined to the isolated individual or the recesses of his consciousness. Man is a social animal and it is inconceivable that the religious dimension of his experience should not be social as well. Regardless of the truth embodied in the doctrine that religion has something to do with what the individual does with his own "solitariness," the fact remains that the existence of religious *community* is the most pervasive trait we encounter in the history of the world's religions. Hermits and solitary ascetics, prophets and reformers there have been, and there is no need to minimize their importance for religion, but these figures always stand out against the background of communities of believers bound together in a common faith. An important feature in the understanding of religion, then, is a clear grasp and appreciation of the community principle in religion, especially its function in providing a means of sharing experience and of making it possible for us to distinguish the perennial from the parochial and evanescent, both in thought and action.

By the community principle is meant a bond of understanding, purpose, and devotion linking together many distinct individuals in such a way that their togetherness can be identified as an enduring whole or unity. Religious community is not primarily the religious institution as a structured organization and center of power in civil society, nor is community the same as "social grouping" within a more encompassing social order. Both of these forms will exist, of course, wherever there is an identifiable religious community, but they are only its embodiments or historical form. Community itself is an ideal relationship based on loyal acknowledgment of a common framework for interpreting human life, a common faith in the religious object, common hopes, and common tasks to be performed in the service of an ideal. The links that bind together many selves in a religious community have a double aspect. On the one hand, they are unifying elements which transcend every individual member of the community and serve to define its limits. On the other hand, the unifying elements must elicit a response from each individual member. Community is not established until the unifying capacity of the common elements is made a reality through loyal acknowledgment by each individual member. In fact, becoming a member of such a community consists precisely in this acknowledgment by the individual that he is committed to and bound by the common faith. Two distinct selves constitute a religious community when each accepts and identifies himself through the faith that both members acknowledge together. Where the community is vital and sensitive to the changing present, the unifying elements will include not only the acceptance of certain beliefs, but tasks and responsibilities as well. The existence of the religious community must be sustained through action as well as thought.

The religious community is based on, and at the same time aids in creating, a transindividual *unity of experience*. This unity represents the funded result of many individual experiences and their interpretation which have been shared and compared for the purpose of separating the well-founded experience from that which is evanescent or incidental. The community provides the medium whereby experience passes beyond individual form and becomes more sharply defined in terms of generic and repeatable features. Consider, for example, the preservation in the memory of the Hebraic community of the cycle of incidents that form the substance of the Joseph story in the Old Testament. The experience of jealousy and revenge which expressed itself in the shameful treatment accorded Joseph by his brothers, and the experience of forgiveness they received when he re-established his community with them despite their treachery, both belong to repeatable human experience. These experiences came to be accepted as a model of what is perennial and repeatable within the experience of each member of the community. The fact that the experience of Joseph and his brothers proved to be continuous with experience had and suffered by others is a major reason for the preservation of the story by the continuing community as part of its sacred past. It is not suggested that the account of Joseph's misfortunes and his forgiveness was itself a "construction" out of many individual experiences. On the contrary, through the community as a medium for sharing and comparing experience, the individual members discover for themselves the representative character of Joseph's experience, since they too experience jealousy and revenge and are capable of showing the redeeming power of forgiveness. The isolated individual may have whatever experiences you please, but he cannot know how representative or perennial they are until he has had an opportunity to share and compare his experience with the experience of others. As a result of the intersection of distinct experiences within a community of shared experience, the idiosyncratic experience gradually becomes distinguished from what is pervasive.

The same point can be illustrated from the experience of St. Paul. When he reported for the early Christian communities his experience of the basic ambiguity he encountered in human life—"The good I would, I do not, and that that I would not, that I do"—he was making available for others a model or representative experience. That his experience was, or is, actually representative or pervasive in the experience of the other members of the community is not to be concluded on the authority of his word alone, nor can its representative character be determined merely by analyzing his report. The fact of shared experience alone makes it possible for others to decide, by attending to their own experience and comparing it with Paul's description, the extent to which he had laid hold of what is well-founded and pervasive as over against the idiosyncratic and parochial.

The idea of a religious community rooted in the acknowledgment by many distinct individuals of a common faith and framework of understanding, and sustained by shared experience, at once invites an instructive parallel. The long history of polemic surrounding the "conflict" between science and religion has managed to obscure a basic similarity between the two, which, if understood, might well serve to remove both misunderstanding and mistrust. If we consider the structure of scientific inquiry, we cannot fail to notice the presence of the community principle at work. Individual investigators and even teams of investigators set to work attempting to answer certain questions or to test specific hypotheses through experimental procedures. The results of such investigation are published through channels that make them available to others whose activity is guided by the same aims and purposes. Only the most naïve, however, suppose that published results are stamped at once as "discoveries" and then entered in some mythical record called "science." What actually happens is very different. The results of original inquiry are first cast into public form and offered for the critical appraisal of a scientific community which extends as far as devotion to the aims and conditions of scientific inquiry can be found. The task is for others to corroborate and validate, or falsify and disprove, the results previously obtained. Such critical testing is accomplished by the reproduction of the original experimental procedures in order to compare the outcomes. The underlying principle of the process is an appeal to shared experience and to an ideal limit or consensus which transcends the experience of any single individual or finite collection of individuals. The isolated experience is exposed to public view where it becomes the task of other inquirers to determine its validity. The goal of this critical process is a convergence of opinion about the claim made in the hypothesis resulting from previous inquiry. Ultimately, that claim is accepted or rejected not by any one individual but by the community of inquirers. Of course, in actual scientific inquiry, especially when large and complex issues are involved, the process is not as simple as has been indicated. In the majority of cases, no clear decision can be reached in a short run and the issue remains in doubt or is regarded as still open and inquiry continues until some agreement is reached. But the actual details are not as important as the fact that the pervasive and well-founded experience is discovered and marked off from the merely idiosyncratic experience by an appeal to a community of shared experience which, through test and comparison, gradually leads to a stable result. The scientific community, no less than the religious, has conditions on which its continued existence depends. The scientific community is rooted in an acknowledgment on the part of all the members of certain binding or unifying elements, the most important of which is a loyalty or devotion to an ideal of truth created by no man, an ideal which is the exclusive property of no individual and no nation.

There are, of course, differences between the two communities which are quite fundamental. Not only do their aims differ, but there is the decisive fact that within the scientific enterprise the requisite critical procedures are such that they can, in principle at least, be reproduced at will according to a recipe. In this fact is found the crucial advantage enjoyed by *experiment* over direct and living experience; experience has its own time and pace and is not manipulable at will. The sort of experience relevant for the religious life is so completely identified with the person who has it that the thought of reproducing it is inappropriate. One cannot simply decide to become an instance of a righteous man unjustly treated by the world for the purpose of discovering what such a situation is like. Nor can one reproduce at will the spirit of forgiveness, the sense of guilt, or the experience of remorse. Despite these differences, however, there is an instructive analogy between the scientific enterprise and the religious community which has hitherto been unjustly ignored. In both cases the singular or isolated experience, subject as it is to the possibility of error, receives whatever critical support it is to get from the testimony of other experiences taking place within a unifying community of thought and experience. The religious community, unfortunately, has often been reluctant to take seriously the critical force of experience and has sought to maintain its faith on authoritarian grounds ignoring the question as to whether religious beliefs can in any sense be supported by experience. A living religion, or rather a religion which hopes to save its life, cannot ultimately afford to avoid the critical test of shared experience. On the contrary, from shared experience comes its life.

Reference thus far to the shared experience of religious community has been to the community of faith associated with historical religious traditions such as Judaism and Christianity. It is clear, however, that a thorough account of the nature of religion must take seriously the fact that there are many distinct religious communities spread throughout the world. For some centuries this fact has either been obscured or minimized, and in the West the prevailing view has been that the Judeo-Christian tradition alone possesses a valid revelation of the divine, while other traditions represent merely humanistic forms of "religion." Modern communication and transportation have so intimately linked the continents that intellectual and cultural parochialism can no longer be sustained. None of the great historic religions can remain consistent with themselves while at the same time continuing to ignore both the challenge and the opportunity offered by the existence of the other religious communities. The time has come for grappling with the *religious* significance of the fact that many religions exist and that some of them, such as the world historical religions, have deep roots in long traditions of experience. Hitherto the historical, anthropological, and cultural aspects of this fact have been emphasized, but little confrontation has taken place at the level of religious meaning.

The existence of many distinct religious communities throughout the world forces us to ask about the possibility of a shared experience that transcends any one of the world religions known at the present time. The possibility in question is not to be confused with the idea of a "world religion" made up of bits and pieces taken from Buddhism, Islam, Christianity, etc. The contemporary world situation precludes such a synthetic religion in any case, and, moreover, it is naïve to suppose that religion can be "created" at will by the engineering intelligence. The question concerns instead the extent of the religious dimension of experience in human life as such. Can there be a shared experience *between* religious communities and not only *within* them? Is there a universal religious situation in which man as man exists, independent of the various factors, ethnic, cultural, economic, etc., that have conditioned the historical form of the world religions? For if the religious dimension of experience forms a generic trait of human existence to be found *wherever* man is found, we shall have to look at the many different world religions with new eyes. Instead of viewing Hinduism, Buddhism, Christianity, and other religions merely as a bewildering collection of different beliefs, forms of ritual, ethics, etc., we shall have to consider the momentous possibility that they represent different *responses* or solutions to the *same problematic situation* in which man finds himself wherever he happens to exist. If this is the case, the enterprise known as "Comparative Religion" is at once revolutionized, for instead of the familiar external catalogue of differences and similarities in belief, ritual, ecclesiastical organization, etc., among the world religions, we shall have a common basis for serious and instructive comparison. We shall view the Buddhist conception of salvation, for example, not simply in its own terms, but as a resolution of the same human predicament to which Christianity addresses itself in offering its own doctrine of salvation.

The question then is, does the religious dimension of human experience, taken on a cosmic scale, have a *structure* of its own which can be delineated and used as an instrument of comparison? A full answer to this question would require another volume, but a step in the direction of an answer can be taken in the form of a general analysis of the religious dimension of experience into three components, which at once define man's problematic situation and the structure of every identifiable religious attempt to resolve that situation. The three components can be called the ideal, the need, and the deliverer, and, as will become clear in the course of the discussion, they can be regarded as an *experiential structure* because they are ingredient in the experience of the individual as well as in the life of the religious community of which he is a member.

To begin with, the concept of structure itself needs to be explained. It should not be necessary to point out that neither the structure of religion nor that of human life exists apart from historical embodiment, but it is important to avoid the supposition that the structure of religion itself represents a universal or "natural" religion freed from detail that is parochial or merely historical. The structure in question has a genuine persistence in all instances of concrete religion and the chief value of seeking to discover it resides in the assistance it provides in understanding religion as a pervasive factor in human life.

Structure is best understood in correlation with function. Structure is contemporaneous pattern or related elements, and function is a temporal development or process in which each structured element plays a particular role. To perform functions, an element must be structured, and a structured element can participate in a process only by performing some function. The two features are correlative and neither can be reduced to the other. A world of pure functioning is impossible since function itself requires structure and a world of pure structure is likewise impossible since every element of a structure has a purpose or is "for" something. The pervasive fact of change does require, however, that the dynamic side of things, the side of function, be regarded as a primary datum; it is through the study of actual functioning that all knowledge of structure is attained. This fact is of special importance for the philosophy of religion, since religion appears as embodied in the most complex set of functions that exists—individual and corporate human life. The only manner in which the structure of religion can be grasped is through its historical manifestation in the lives of individuals and in the religious community or church.

Religion, wherever we find it, manifests a threefold structure that can be set forth in generic terms. These terms can be further specified for interpreting a given religious tradition and they can be used as a powerful tool in the task of understanding the many world religions and of introducing order into what might otherwise appear to be but a chaos of historical information. *First*, religion demands an ideal or religious object that is at once the ground and goal of all existence. As ground this object is the source of all that is and constitutes the reason why there is anything at all; as goal this object defines the ultimate destiny of all that is, especially the ideal being of man and what he may become. *Second*, religion lives in the conviction that natural existence or life as we find it is separated from that ideal or religious object by some flaw or defect. Contrary to popular belief, religion does not thrive on an undiluted idealism or optimism; high and profound religion reveals a vivid sense of the distorted or broken character of existence and of some deep need on the part of man not only for the form of life manifested in the ideal or religious object, but for the removal of the flaw that infects his being and separates him from what he essentially is or was meant to be. Finally, there is a *third* element, which takes the form of the deliverer, or power that overcomes the need or flaw in existence and is able to establish the ideal on the far side, so to speak, of broken or distorted existence. The three elements, then, that go to make up the structure of the religious dimension are the ideal, or religious object, the defect in existence, or need, and the saving power, or the deliverer. Prior to the interpretation of these elements in terms appropriate for a particular religious tradition, they remain general and open to some variety of content.

Every historical religion and a considerable number of substitutes that have functioned as religions can be shown to exhibit the structure just indicated. A clear description of this structure depends on the clarity with which the three basic concepts can be set forth and related to actual religion. Prior to this analysis it is necessary to understand the internal connections between the three elements and to see that these connections enter essentially into their meaning. The nature of the ideal serves to interpret the task of the deliverer by making clear what form of existence the deliverer must establish. The nature of the need clarifies both the ideal and the task of the deliverer by contrast. The flaw that separates us from the ideal makes us more vividly aware of the life abundant that we do not yet possess, and it shows us clearly what it is that the deliverer has to overcome. Finally, the deliverer shows forth the ideal as that which is really real despite the reality of the flaw that separates man from it.

The relations between the structural elements are not only logical in character, but ontological and temporal as well. Ideally, the religious life should include the temporal or historical character of actual existence. We should begin with a vision of the ideal from which should follow the sense of being finite and unclean in comparison with the ideal, leading on in turn to the quest for the deliverer. In view of the variety in human individuality, the ideal logical pattern will not be repeated exactly in every case; the important point, however, is not mere conformity to a pattern but rather the acknowledgment of the historical nature of life. It is extremely doubtful whether a religious tradition can contain the truth about human life in its day-to-day movement unless it acknowledges the reality of time and relates the progress of human life to the cosmic process of redemption. For those religious traditions in which the dynamic character of concrete life is lost, redemption becomes a timeless affair that seems without relevance to ordinary life and experience. When the redemptive process is thought to take place entirely apart from historical life with all of its tragedy and distortion—as indeed it does for some forms of Hinduism and Buddhism and Christianity when it stresses only *Heilsgeschichte*—actual life is abandoned or it becomes no more than an incident in a myth of cosmic proportions. This undesirable consequence is avoided if we view the structure of religion not as a timeless pattern but as marking out a progression of the religious life—a movement, that is, from a vision of the ideal to the awareness of the need that separates us from it and on to the quest for the deliverer.

In order to employ the three structural concepts to describe the universal structure of religion, it becomes necessary to set them forth in abstraction from what is distinctive of any singular religion. We must not conclude, however, that emphasis on the universal structure necessitates the loss of what is distinctive and thus essential in the singular religious traditions. On the contrary, the opposition often envisaged between the universal and the singular is a false opposition, for it is only through the use of universal conceptions which make possible significant critical comparisons between singulars of the same kind that we are able to discover and express clearly what is distinctive of the singular phenomenon. We may begin, for example, with the concept of deliverer as universal and then select from each religious tradition the element or feature in it that functions as deliverer, compare the several cases, and finally arrive at an understanding of the utter distinctness of each singular religion in the respect chosen for comparison. Such comparison by means of a structural concept, far from obscuring what is distinctive in the singular, enables us instead to grasp it more clearly just because we now know it through explicit contrast with other examples of the same kind.

Ideal. The ideal is the central element in all religion since it comprehends within its meaning the meaning of the religious object itself. As a consequence, the ideal takes on a twofold meaning corresponding to the two aspects of the religious object—ground or standard guiding and judging life on the one hand, and goal or fulfillment of life on the other. In relation to the religious object, ultimate concern as experienced by the individual takes on a double meaning. There is a concern by the self for knowledge of its present status, the ground upon which it lives, and there is a concern directed away from the present self and toward a perfection of life which everyone but the most complacent person knows that he does not possess. A present imperfection can, however, be apprehended only through a *contrast-effect* in which the actual situation is compared with the ideal. In the legend of Job, for example, we can readily see the function of such contrast. The traditional conception of God called for prosperous life for the righteous and punishment for the wicked; Job's condition, both as a model of the righteous man and yet as one who suffers and does not prosper, stands in sharp contrast with the ideal as then conceived. The same point can be seen in Augustine's claim in *De Beata Vita* that the self cannot know its present condition without a standard of perfection by which to judge. By consulting the ideal, the person gains knowledge both of his present state and of what he is meant to become.

Every religion contains more or less clear teaching concerning the ideal or religious object in the dual sense of standard or truth about human life in the world and of goal expressing the ultimate purpose of life. It is characteristic of most religion that it is realistic, because it views human life as standing under the judgment of a truth in contrast with which all other forms of life are regarded as defective and as carrying within themselves the seeds of destruction. This truth about life is revealed in the nature of the ideal and is regarded as a present perfection not entirely dependent upon a process of realization in the future. As standard and truth about life within the world, the ideal provides the guiding principle of morality. Understood as already embodying the final form of life, the ideal exemplifies the properly religious meaning of life since it takes us beyond what we are *to do* and makes plain what we are *to be*.

Christianity has a clear view of the ideal in the sense in which it is here understood. The New Testament reaffirms the one God of earlier Biblical religion, with the radical added belief that the final nature of God is found in the figure of Jesus as Christ. In Christ the concept of God as loving-kindness and as merciful, so much emphasized by the Old Testament prophets and so vividly expressed in the later chapters of the Book of Isaiah, is brought to completion in the form of sacrificial love. The justice of the divine nature is also preserved in the New Testament picture of God, for the coming of the final manifestation of God is itself regarded as a form of judgment. Justice, however, is seen as comprehended within the divine love since the element of vengeance is eliminated and replaced by the idea of the divine persuasion aiming at preserving the life rather than bringing about the death of the sinner.

From the Christian perspective, the ideal appears as a center of understanding that transcends the world while also dwelling within it. The divine nature is seen as providing the clue to the truth about human life in the world, including the standard that should determine the relations between man and man. The writer of the First Epistle of John expresses the point in a forceful way—"If a man say, I love God, and hate his brother, he is a liar." * For Christianity, what we have here been calling the ideal incorporates still more. It presents not only the divine nature and the law of life in the world, but it includes a

* I John iv. 20 (RSV); the great commandment of Matt. xxii. 37ff., Luke x. 27 ff. is, of course, presupposed.

doctrine of the ultimate purpose of life and a vision of the perfect life. In Christianity, the doctrine of the Kingdom of God and of the life that is described as eternal, represent that part of the ideal from which we discover the true end of man. Much of the direct teaching of Jesus concerns the Kingdom, the quality of life it demands, its nature, its relation to the world of time and history, and its final consumation in God. The Kingdom is described as a community of persons whose relations with each other are governed by the principle of the divine αγάπη. This community of selves constitutes the ideal of man's life and the quality of life envisaged is the "eternal life" of Christian belief.* The so-called "farewell prayer" of Jesus as recorded in John contains the classical description of eternal life: "And this is the life eternal, that they should know thee the only true God . . ." (John xvii. 3). The knowledge of God, that is, with all the implications of loving and willing that the term connotes, defines eternal life, the perfection of human existence.

Central as the ideal is for every religion, it does not exhaust religion. For, though the ideal be the final reality, religion is incurably realistic in the sense that it points us to a deep awareness that, as we presently are and stand, we are separated from the ideal. Each religious tradition has its own diagnosis of what we earlier called the need, the obstacle, flaw, deficiency that must be overcome if the ideal is to be established in its fullness. A poet has written, "Between the promise and the fulfillment falls the shadow"; this shadow finds its place in the structure of religion as the concept of the need.

Need. In view of the fact that religion is so frequently associated with hope and triumph it may seem strange to assert that the concept of need—the dark side of religious insight—is, in many respects, the most important of the three concepts. De-

* See in addition to the many passages in the synoptic Gospels, especially the so-called "parables of the kingdom," the many references to the Kingdom of God, e.g. Rom. xiv. 17, I Cor. iv. 20, vi. 9–10, Col. iv. 11, II Thess. 1. 5.

spite the seeming incongruity, its importance remains. Between the ideal as it stands before man in the form of a goal that has, in fact, not yet been realized, and its final realization, stands the need as a stubborn and intractable obstacle. The religious perspective, that is, cannot be summed up in the complacent claim that all is well with the world, that the ideal is real regardless of the tragic distortion of human life. On the contrary, all religions of scope and depth are filled with a clear sense of the negative judgment on existence. Life as it exists—the life of the "natural" man—is distorted; it is not as it ought to be because it harbors within itself some flaw or deep need that has to be met with and overcome before we can speak confidently of the triumph of the ideal. Far from being the complacent celebration of a transcendent goodness existing above and beyond historical life, the religious perspective forces us to acknowledge the reality of evil and of some deep-seated obstacle that stands between us as we naturally exist and the attainment of the ideal. As will become clear, the concept of the need provides us with a powerful tool for the comparative interpretation of the world religions. When we can specify exactly where a given religion finds the need, and what nature it assigns to the flaw in existence, we have a clue not only to its diagnosis of the human predicament, but also to its understanding of the task set for the deliverer or the power that is to effect the resolution.

Although attention has already been called to the temporal aspect of the structure of religion and its reflection of the movement of human life, it is not literally the case that the awareness of the need falls neatly between the awareness of the ideal and the quest for the deliverer in the case of every individual person. A general description cannot hope to express adequately the variety to be found in individual experience. It is clear, nevertheless, that the awareness of the need depends upon confrontation by the ideal, and a serious acknowledgment of the reality of the need is required if we are to have the quest for the deliverer. In this sense the need does fall between the other two elements in the structure.

To the extent to which the self knows the imperfect character of its present life, it can be said that the self begins to be aware of the need. The person, that is, becomes aware, perhaps vaguely and dimly at first, of an incongruity, an incompleteness, and a lack of satisfaction within himself. The first sense of the need corresponds to the common experience of *feeling that* a situation is unsatisfactory, without having at the same time any clear *understanding* of exactly *what* is the cause of the deficiency. The first sense of the need is negative; it appears largely as the lack or absence of something, like the experience of a void unaccompanied by a clear grasp of what would fill it or overcome the emptiness.

When the ideal becomes more explicit—usually in a vivid way through example, as in the model set by the Buddha or the pattern of love exemplified in Christ—the contrast between the norm and present life begins to define itself more clearly. As the awareness of the gulf between the actual and the ideal becomes more insistent, the sense of need becomes more and more acute and, as a result, it assumes a different form. The need now presents itself as a positive obstacle; it appears no longer as a "privation" or deficiency. The need now takes on an active and powerful existence, the overcoming of which becomes a matter of serious concern.

When the need is finally grasped as a positive power separating the person from the ideal, a new distinction becomes appropriate. It is the distinction between the need as an obstacle which can, in principle, be overcome or removed by man himself as he now exists in the world, and the need as something that cannot, in its own nature, be overcome by the same being who has the need. The internal connection between the three structural concepts becomes especially clear at this point. The nature and office of the deliverer depends to a very large extent on the sense in which the need is understood. For it is the task of the deliverer—whatever precise form it may take—to overcome the need and establish the ideal. It is, therefore, crucial whether the one who has the need is able to function as his own deliverer or whether the deliverer must be another, existing above and beyond man and capable of performing what man in his natural existence is unable to accomplish. Several possibilities present themselves. At one extreme is the humanistic view, according to which the being in need still retains sufficient resources within himself to overcome the need through some form of discipline and effort. At the other extreme is the view of radical discontinuity, according to which the being in need is so radically separated from the ideal that no basis whatever exists within the nature of the being in need from which the process of recovery or redemption is possible. Between these extremes, that of total continuity and total discontinuity between man and the ideal, other views are possible that would seek to do justice to both elements while accepting neither extreme position as the final truth.

The differing interpretations are of central importance not only for the theory of man, but in relation to the concept of the deliverer. The office of the deliverer must be understood in relation to the being who is to be delivered, and to what it is that he is to be delivered from. Where man is seen as, in principle, capable of redeeming himself, i.e. where the need is regarded as something that is pliable or respondent to human effort, the deliverer inevitably becomes no more than an *example* of what man would have to be and to do in order to achieve his own salvation. On the other hand, if the need is understood as involving a recalcitrant factor, something that resists human ingenuity and power, the deliverer has a far different office. In this latter case, the deliverer is no longer merely an examplar, but must become *a source of power* available to the being in need, a source of power that man is unable to provide for himself from his own resources alone.

These differences in understanding concern the precise nature and office of the deliverer; they do not alter the fact that the deliverer remains a necessary element in the structure of religion generally. For, as was previously pointed out, religion always contains, within its interpretations and items of belief, a diagnosis of man and the world aimed at revealing the flaw in existence separating us from the ideal. The grand strategy of the enduring world religions has been to diagnose that flaw and then to point to some form of deliverer able to overcome it. The decisive fact is that the major religions have not agreed in their diagnosis and consequently they differ in their view of what sort of deliverer is required for making up the deficiency. After brief comment on the concept of the deliverer, I shall propose a threefold comparison illustrating these differences and at the same time showing how the theory of a general structure of religion provides us with a powerful conceptual tool for finding patterns of intelligibility among the world religions and of making critical comparisons. For if human life itself has a universal structure relatively independent of ethnic and cultural conditions, it might then be possible to discuss the question of which of the major religions possesses the most faithful and relevant account of the human predicament and of its resolution.

Deliverer. Much has already been said to indicate the meaning of this concept. The deliverer has two aspects: a function or office to be performed and filled, and a specific nature that makes this operation possible. The task of the deliverer is, as we have said, to overcome the need and establish the ideal in the face of distorted existence. Whether the deliverer need be identical with the ideal, as in the case of Christianity, or an instrument through which the redeeming process is accomplished, will depend on several factors. It is well, however, to notice that the deliverer need not be a person. Unfortunately, the term itself connotes a person and perhaps another term should be found that does not have this restriction attached to it. For in actual fact, the deliverer has assumed a variety of forms: in some religions it is knowledge that delivers, in others it is a law, and in still others, a sacred discipline. Moreover, in the case of some of the secular substitutes for religion, the deliverer has been a political system or even the course of history itself. But if what we have called the structure of religion is to be adequate for the interpretation of religion wherever it appears, variety must be allowed for in the structural concepts themselves. Christianity views the deliverer as assuming the form of a person, whereas other religions do not, but there will always be a counterpart for the deliverer in every tradition.*

The explanatory value of the structure of religion can best be seen, not from further general analysis, but from actual comparison. Let us consider, in brief compass, the conception of the need and the deliverer to be found in three traditions—the Vedanta form of Hinduism, Buddhism in its nontheistic form, and Christianity. A comparison involving so much in a short space need not be regarded as superficial, since we need attend only to certain precisely selected features.

The Vedanta says that what separates man from the realization of the true self, that is, the need, is a misapprehension of the true nature of things. The need is located in a failure to *understand* reality as it really is. The true self (*Atman*) is that underlying unity most closely approximated in human experience by the dreamless sleeper who is effectively beyond the distractions caused by the separateness of things and by finite individuality. There is a tendency in this position to regard the fact of individuality itself as the obstacle standing between the self and its realization of the truth. What needs to be overcome is this mistaken view of things as finite, individual, separate, and sundered from each other. What is demanded as the deliverer is knowledge, a form of insight which, once attained, teaches the believer that individuality or discontinuity in reality is not the final truth and that the true self cannot be found among the items of the plurality. If the need appears as the defect (including partiality of insight) inherent in finite individuality itself, the deliverer must assume the form that overcomes the partial in-

* It is interesting to note moreover, that the classical Christian theologians were not insensitive to the problem of the exact form the deliverer must assume, which is precisely why Anselm's well-known question, *Cur Deus Homo*?, has continued to be of theological interest.

sight and the limitations of individual existence. The deliverer is itself knowledge and insight, the insight that individuality is not an ultimate form of existence and that the true self is identical with the *Atman*.

In Buddhism as it can be derived from the ancient legends that were passed on concerning the original experience of the Buddha and his illumination, we find a different diagnosis of man's plight and a different interpretation of the need. Once again the quest is for the true self and the proper path toward self-realization. The need, however, appears not as a form of ignorance or misunderstanding, but rather as the boundlessness of desire. In some of the early tales, the Buddha specifically refuses to answer speculative questions about the state of Nirvana, but insists instead that his task is to disclose the cause of suffering and to show that it consists in the ever-recurring cycle of desire, limited satisfaction, renewed desire, and so on without end. The need is, therefore, for a way of overcoming the formlessness of desire and of subjecting it to discipline. The function of the Buddha as deliverer is to offer the illumination he has gained, an illumination that teaches, theoretically, about desire as the cause of suffering and, practically, about the noble eightfold path that leads to life. Whitehead, in his most instructive comparison between Buddhism and Christianity, claimed that, whereas in Christianity Christ gives his life in performing his role, the Buddha gives only a doctrine. This claim is only partially true. The Buddha does not give himself in the fashion Christians understand the life of Christ to be given, but we must not overestimate the contrast. The Buddha gives a doctrine, to be sure, but we must not neglect the sense in which Buddhists take inspiration from the *actual attainment* of the Buddha, the fact of his illumination and of his example for others. Moreover, the Buddha postpones his own fulfillment in order to return and bring enlightenment to others.

It is of the greatest moment that the Buddhist conception of the need is not entirely an affair of knowledge. Desire, that is to say, cannot be overcome in its destructive effects through the attainment of an insight alone. Since the defect is located more nearly in the will and in human striving, a contemplative insight will not suffice to dispel the need. Insight and understanding are there, but something more is required, something closer to moral wisdom, and the power to desire and to act in accordance with the noble virtues. The Buddha functions as deliverer both through the moral insight he attains and through the fact of his actual achievement, which shows that it is possible for man to reach the good life.

If the Vedanta finds the need in the partiality and imperfection of individuality and Buddhism in the destructive force of desire that is without form, the Judeo-Christian tradition finds it more deeply rooted in the *freedom* of man. The need does not in a literal sense belong to the necessary structure of natural existence, but rather to the capacity of a free being to make himself his own end and thus to deny the sovereignty of the true God. Here the need resides neither in the structure of being individual or separate, nor in desire as a part of natural being, but in the capacity of a free being to deny God and the divine law. The need is internal to the individual, but it does not at all consist in the fact that he *is* individual.

The task of the deliverer is to provide a norm for man's freedom and a source of power to perform without at the same time denying that freedom by reducing man to the status of an object or thing. The deliverer is to save man from the self-destructive consequences of his own misuse of freedom and to make possible a measure of the eternal quality of life envisaged in the ideal.

It is not difficult to see from this brief comparison that the traditions in question exhibit a common structure, directing their attention to an ideal, diagnosing a need or flaw, and proposing a resolution in the form of a deliverer. It is equally clear that the three do not understand the three elements in the same way; each has its own understanding of the tragic flaw and of the resolution that enables us to overcome it. But, viewed from the standpoint of a common structure, the differing traditions do not seem so strange. Not that we shall pass lightly over differences in the interests of merely diplomatic agreements; on the contrary, the differences stand out vividly by comparison, but these differences now appear within the framework of a common endeavor. We are better able to consider the relative merits of the different diagnoses offered and the possibility of overcoming the needs defined by the deliverers that appear. By this we come ultimately to a clearer understanding of where we all stand.

Epilogue: Religion and Secularization

The dominant fact about Western civilization since the era of the Renaissance and Reformation, a fact profoundly affecting every sphere of life, but especially the sphere of the religious, is the fact of *secularization*. The term itself is likely to evoke powerful responses of approval or disapproval even before there is a clear understanding of the fundamental historical situation to which it points. For some, "secularization" will be honorific in its meaning and for others, pejorative; perhaps it is naïve to suppose that the term can have a purely "neutral" use which involves no more than pointing to the facts themselves. Whether this is the case or not, good sense dictates our assuming that there is such a neutral sense and beginning with certain recurrent features of contemporary life in the representative nations of the West in order to focus attention on what constitutes the phenomenon of secularization. The proper evaluation of that phenomenon, and especially the response to it that is called for from the religious standpoint, can be postponed until we have some grasp of what secularization is and means.

It is not without point to begin the discussion with an etymological fact about such terms as "secular," "secularism," and their relatives. The dominant connotation of these terms is that of having transactions in and with the "world," understood as a physical environment and a cultural habitat. A temporal as well as spatial reference is involved, so that "secular" means the present state of things as part of an ongoing process of development, as well as what concerns earthly, natural, or "profane" life taking place in some geographical portion of the world.* The connotation of being in and grappling with the "world" both as spatial and temporal order helps point the way to an understanding of "secular" and "secularization" as these terms apply to our present cultural situation and to the course of its development over the past four hundred years. Although, as will become clear, a complex, dialectical relation obtains between the Western religious tradition and the secular world that has emerged from the breakdown of medieval Christendom, this fact should not prompt the conclusion that secularization stands to religion as the "enemy" or even that there is an irreconcilable opposition between them. That conclusion has caused, and can still cause, great damage.

What, in terms both of human consciousness and the structure of modern life, does secularization mean? The answer can be given in its most concise form by means of five outstanding traits that not only mark life in the most highly developed nations of the West, but which now fire the imagination and spark the wills of countless millions in those lands we have come to describe as underdeveloped. These traits are *autonomy*, expressed individually as freedom and ethnically as national independence or the right of self-determination; *technology*, or industrialization which means science transformed into human power over the environment and even man himself; *voluntarism*, with its closely associated individualism acting as the drive to control recalcitrant forces both in the inner depths of man and the temporal stretches of human history; *temporalism*, or a sense of urgency expressing itself with sharp focus on present existence and the immediate, and a corresponding lack of concern for the abiding, the time-spanning, and the long-range goal.

* See A. Souter, *A Glossary of Later Latin to 600 A.D.* (Oxford, 1949), for the entries, *saecularis* (κοσμικός), *saeculum* (ἀιών, κόsμος), p. 361.

The fifth trait, which is closely connected with the preceding, is one for which it is difficult to find an adequate term; the basic feature is a concern for art, for the senses, for free self-expression, coupled with a feeling of relief wherever it is possible to break out of conventional patterns. This trait may be called "aestheticism" if the term is not understood in a basically derogatory sense, and if it is taken to include the two elements that must always be comprehended by art, namely, an appeal to significant sensible form and an expression of "free play" indicating that the system in which we live has relaxed its demands upon us.*

These hallmarks of secularization will be seen as having a double-barreled character. On the one hand, they exist as forms of consciousness structuring and determining the minds, the attitudes, and the spirit both of individuals and of groups; and on the other, they find their being as objective forms of society structuring and determining the lives of nations and the course of modern history. To apply a pungent distinction borrowed from Peirce, the marks of secularization are not only in our minds, but in our muscles; they exist both in the manner in which we think and view the world and in our overt transactions with our environment and fellow human beings. Through our behavior secularization takes on an objective and public shape in the form of the society and the culture which the modern world has produced.

If, now, we can describe these five traits in greater detail, we shall have a better understanding of what secularization means and the form of life it embodies. It is to this form of life and society that the religious outlook must be related. The question is, What is the proper response to be made by the adherents of the Western religious traditions to the fact of secularization in modern life? In posing this question, a word of caution is required: although it cannot be denied that the drive toward secularization

* The "free play" aspect of aestheticism is the antithesis of the responsibility that is entailed by autonomy, and also of the discipline and the strenuous life imposed by voluntarism and individualism.

often in fact meant struggle against the religious standpoint, especially in its positive and authoritarian form, great harm will come from supposing that there is an irreconcilable opposition between secularization and religion in the sense that the only response possible for either is to condemn the other. That supposition confuses the situation and disguises its true nature. The major problem posed by secularization is not new; that problem is the ancient one of how religion is to be related to the "world," and how life *in* the world is to be related to man's concern for the holy ground of his existence expressed in and through the religious dimension of experience. Therefore the initial supposition that religion and secularization stand to each other simply as enemies misses the depth of the problem and actually stands in the way of any progress toward a solution. For if we knew before we analyzed the actual situation that the religious standpoint and the secularized form of life were totally disparate and that each of us is faced with the choice of deciding for one or the other, there would be no need to inquire further. The situation, however, is more complex and, as I shall suggest, more "dialectical" than simple opposition can encompass. The proper course is to return to an analysis of secularization as a prelude to arriving at an understanding of the way in which the religious standpoint is to be related to contemporary secularized life. In this way we not only do greater justice to the full dimensions of the problem, but, in addition, we reinforce the sound philosophical principle that, in confronting any complex, we *first* distinguish its elements and *then* relate the elements distinguished to each other in various intelligible ways.

AUTONOMY

No trait in secularized life is more important and, indeed, more prominent than that of antonomy. Its meaning, stated classically by Kant in the eighteenth century, is primarily self-determination or self-legislation and the rejection of all forms of subjection to an authority that appears to us as strange or alien. The point can be seen most clearly in the spheres of political and religious life. The challenge brought against the two classical foundations of political power—hereditary succession and religious sanction or "divine right"—which we associate principally with the political philosophy of the Enlightenment, was brought in the name of man as a rational and autonomous being. Such a creature, it was argued (in different ways by such diverse thinkers as Locke, Rousseau, and Kant), possesses a dignity which is inconsistent with his being subject to a political power which he can in no way recognize as an expression of his own will. To be subject to such an alien power was regarded in Kant's language, as "heteronomy," or control by the "other" who stands over against and does not express one's own self. The dignity of the free and rational being demands, not freedom *from* law and authority, but rather a political system in which the two are ultimately self-imposed through institutions and devices which represent the will and the nature of the being who is subject to that political system. The demand for autonomy as an ideal, therefore, was not essentially the demand to be an arbitrary individual who is a law unto himself and thus beyond the reach of all authority, but rather the demand that political power not be the imposition of an alien will which neither expresses man's own will nor acknowledges his being as a rational and free creature. Authority and the restraint entailed by the exercise of political power in any form can be accepted by the autonomous person, if, first, he sees his own will represented in it, and, second, the form assumed by that authority is such that it acknowledges the peculiar nature of a free being. This means that man is not to be regarded as an object among other objects who may be subjected to law or determined after the fashion of a star or a stone. Man indeed needs to be governed, but the governing power must be responsive to his own will and must govern in accordance with the fact that the being to be governed has a peculiar nature of his own—namely, a nature of reason and freedom. All paradoxes of political power and its exercise follow from that fact.

Similarly, in the religious sphere the demand for autonomy originally meant an attack upon ecclesiastical authority considered as an alien power determining a man's religious and moral obligations without concern for his conscience and the exercise of his reason. Here the problem was complicated by the fact that the heteronomous or alien power was identified not only as the ecclesiastical power of the positive religion, but in theological terms as well. The demand for autonomy called into question the conception of God as an arbitrary despot whose commands, no matter how difficult they might be to understand in terms of human reason and experience, must be obeyed without hesitation or question. Tillich expressed the point in an arresting way when he declared that "We cannot be obedient to the commands of a stranger, even if he is God." The spirit of both Kant and of the Reformation are at once revivified in this utterance. Insofar as man, despite his capacity for evil and injustice, is essentially a creature of freedom and reason, he cannot consistently be commanded as if he were an inanimate object or thing. He cannot, moreover, subject himself with sincerity to a law that is entirely beyond the scope of his understanding. Nor can he manifest love to a lawgiver whose authority merely stands over against him as an alien power connected in no essential way with his own. Autonomy finds its crucial test in the sphere of religion because the free being is led to question the divine ground of his own existence and to ask for an intelligible moral law and an intelligible God.

Autonomy in every sphere carries with it the need for responsibility. A being who is going to be self-determining must also be answerable, not only for his deeds, but for the ideal self which he chooses as a guide for the conduct of his life. Autonomy therefore carries with it a burden of considerable proportion; that burden is the price of man's freedom to be a free being and to demand that he be treated in accordance with his nature as such a being. Autonomous man, if he is consistent, must eschew all forms of reductive explanation of his behavior that tend to diminish the extent of his responsibility either through his physical constitution or the conditions imposed by the society in which he lives.

Autonomy in its extreme expression is seen most clearly in the free being of secularized existentialism. This contemporary position is the final stage in a long development that makes manifest the several forms autonomy may assume. In the period of Kant, the autonomy for which he argued was informed by the ideal of a universal human nature transcending cultural and parochial limits. The continuity of human nature was thought to have, as a corollary, a community of free beings, expressed, for example, in Kant's conception of a kingdom of ends. Although Kant believed that in stressing man's freedom he was attacking the idea that man had a fixed or substantial nature which merely unfolds in time, his conception has gradually come to be regarded as too "substantial" in character. The social or community principle implied in Kant's view of a universal human nature has been lost. The contemporary ideal of autonomous man is an individualistic one in the extreme. The paradigm is the man of secularized existentialism—he has no "essence" preceding his existence, which is to say, his freedom; he stands alone as *this* unduplicable individual who, if he is to be authentic, can rely neither on his community nor his past, but must seek to be wholly self-determined in the sense of realizing himself in and through the projects which he alone can project. On this view, man *is* his freedom and since each individual exists only in the authentic exercise of that freedom, each individual is alone. And, as we shall see, at its best, this form of autonomy is a heroic call for total responsibility and, at its worst, it degenerates into an irresponsible individualism of self-expression in which there is no place for community and no concern for that sharing of burdens without which neither social nor political life is possible.

TECHNOLOGY AND INDUSTRIALIZATION

There is no need here to repeat the by now familiar truths and truisms about the impact of industrial and technological revolutions on modern life. The political, social, and economic dimensions of these revolutions have been exhaustively analyzed. What is needed is a grasp of the philosophical and even religious meaning behind our technological society. Technology is the concrete evidence for the truth of the doctrine that "knowledge is power"; technology represents the cultivation of nature, together with the attempt to gain control over as much of it as we are able; finally, technology means the exploitation of nature and the reduction of the natural environment to a collection of pure objects that have no interiority or autonomy of their own but exist only as material for man's creative will. Technology and industrialization reveal themselves most clearly as traits of secularization in one point—they express man's conviction that the earth, the world (including heights, depths, and extents still to be revealed) *can be made into an abiding habitation for man* so that it is no longer necessary to look beyond, behind, beneath that world for a further source of fulfillment. In religious language, the quest for the city "which hath foundations, and whose maker and builder is God" seems fruitless. In any case, such a quest is superfluous since the earth, transformed by the creative ingenuity of man, can be made into a permanent home. As the treasures of the earth are found and made available, man's needs and wants are satisfied in an abundant and clearly affluent society. Secularization means the transformation of the earthly city into a secure and self-sufficient habitation so that one need no longer seek the hidden city, the city envisaged by the eyes of religious faith.

In the most comprehensive sense, technology and industrialization provide three forms of applying knowledge and mechanical skill to the development of nature. First, there is *cultivation* of natural resources, the discovery of the structures and potentialities of things for the purpose of co-operating as fully as possible with these natural structures and thus achieving the most fruitful and abundant results. Second, there is the anticipation and *control* of the natural environment. An element of control is, of course, involved in all forms of man's effort to develop nature, but whereas cultivation implies co-operation with natural processes, control means a purposive redirection of processes and an attempt to thwart those developments which are injurious to man or inimical to his progress. In the cultivation of the soil, for example, we seek to increase the yield of a given crop per acre and we do this by accelerating and enchancing natural processes. In the fight to control and ultimately prevent disease we seek to thwart certain processes or to eliminate certain outcomes. The destruction of a natural process, such as the elimination of an insect pest or the killing of a virus by chemical means, represents control of the natural environment. No absolutely precise distinction can be drawn between co-operating with, or "following" nature, and intervening in natural processes so as to control them in "unnatural" ways. The subtle and extended controversy over birth control illustrates the point nicely. The thwarting of conception under certain circumstances implies explicit control, but it is difficult to show that any one technique for accomplishing this end is "more natural" than any other. The rhythm method, the diaphragm, and the birth control pill represent different means of thwarting conception, but it is difficult (if not impossible) to show that one is "more natural" (in the sense of co-operating with natural processes) than another. It is quite likely that, given the often unpredictable character of man's sexual drive, the rhythm method will appear in some situations as quite "unnatural" and the use of the pill will allow for greater "co-operation" with the natural processes involved. The point here, however, is not to enter on a full-scale discussion of birth control, but only to use the issue as an illustration of the difficulty we confront in attempting to draw a *knife-edge distinction* between what I have called cultivation and control. That *some* distinction, nevertheless, needs to be drawn becomes clear when we consider the third feature of technology and industrialization, namely, the *exploitation* of the natural environment. Cultivation implies a recognition of some autonomy for nature over against man—there are given natural structures and processes with which man must reckon whether he wants to or not. Control, on the other hand, implies that the autonomy of nature is not absolute. If man is to have dominion over nature—and in aiming at this result, secularized society is following an ancient biblical maxim—he cannot accept the absolute autonomy of the environment. Man must seek to thwart whatever is hostile to him in nature and to neutralize it as far as possible. Exploitation of the environment, however, represents the process in which the autonomy of nature is denied in every respect. In exploitation, nature is reduced entirely to the status of an inert object, completely subject to the will of man. When man exploits nature, when he destroys the landscape with hideous signs which do not tell the truth, or when he literally reduces acres of virgin forest to paper on which to print a message which does not edify, he is treating nature in the same tyrannical fashion in which he himself was treated by the despot God who commanded him to obey as if he were no more than a grain of sand or a piece of timber.

Exploitation, which is essentially the subjection of everything—man as well as the natural environment—to human will and desire, means the use of something which is in no essential way controlled by the nature of the thing that is used. Exploitation represents a final stage in the process of developing the world as the scene of man's established existence, because it means the total victory of human will and ingenuity over the environing medium of life. The attitude displayed is characteristic of secularization, for when man's life is seen as wholly "mundane" and as falling entirely within the world, concern for what transcends the world fades away and the holy depth of life becomes obscured. In the process, the natural world itself ceases to be an expression of a transcendent power and thus comes to be at the mercy of man in the sense that he feels entirely free to explain it or treat it as if it had no being of its own. There are, however, good reasons to believe that exploitation is a distorted and corrupted response, and does not belong *necessarily* to secularization. Cultivation and control might, when coupled with wisdom, express the true limits of man's development of nature. But exploitation is an obvious fact and it poses a major problem in man's attempt to make the universe into a final and secure habitation.

VOLUNTARISM AND INDIVIDUALISM

The drive toward autonomy and the development of the environment through technological ingenuity reveal modern man as essentially a creature of will. Although according to ancient tradition, the Word was in the beginning, it is the mark of secularization to regard the *deed*, the expression of determination and resolution, as the foundation of all life. Man is to be that unique being who shall control his own destiny and to succeed calls for something more effective than thought or reflection. The high value placed on action shows itself in an immediate (but not very profound) way in "activism" or the conviction that the only genuine contribution to be made to a cause is that of an immediate agitation or display of power. This surface demonstration so evident today in bewildered and disoriented youth points to the underlying voluntarism of modern secularization. If an ontology were involved, we could readily say what it would be: *To be is to be in action.* The extent to which the pragmatic tradition in American thought has contributed to this outlook has long been recognized. What has not often been noticed, however, is the role played by voluntarism in producing a high degree of individualization, something which leads in turn to individualism and the fragmentation of human life.

There is nothing about me as an individual which is more clearly, certainly and unmistakably my own than my *deeds*.

What I do, what I am responsible for, remain irrevocably my own. The structure of my thought has a definitely universal character about it, and the more closely my knowledge approaches the truth of any matter, the less distinguishable am I as an individual. For this reason science is a truly universal and impersonal affair, arriving at truths which no one can be said to "own." Although my feelings—especially my pains—have often been regarded as the most "private" feature of myself, and the factor which marks me off as *this* person in contradistinction from all others, the fact remains that I have my psychological and physiological structure in common with other men. When we come to action, however, the picture alters. No one can will for another; no one other than myself can do the deed which I am obligated to do, and no one but myself can be responsible for the deed I have done.* There is, to be sure, a structure to human action, and acts do fall into classes so that we are able to describe and evaluate them in general terms, but there is a unique relation between myself and my deed as well as a sense that just that deed could have been done by no other. The sense of obligation to act, and the awareness of responsibility for having acted, both focus my attention upon myself as a bounded creature who is a source of effects in the world which I alone can bring about. It is the self-reflexive character of voluntarism which leads to individualism,† for purposive action requires that I consult myself in order to devise a plan and then remind myself that I am the one who has to carry it out.

Secularized life is highly individualized life. It may assume collectivistic forms for the purpose of defending common interests

* The issue here does not concern the vicarious suffering of atonement or the sharing of guilt within a community of faith. The point is simply to show how the voluntaristic outlook leads to individualism.

† It is necessary to make a clear distinction between (1) The recognition of *individual* freedom and autonomy in opposition to absolutistic collectivism such as fascism represents, and (2) *individualism*, or social nominalism in which community is regarded as essentially a fiction and the forms of togetherness are seriously undermined if not entirely rejected.

in the many power struggles of modern competitive life. But secularization is individualistic and drives against the establishment of community. The phenomenon is well illustrated in the "secular city" where gigantic collections of people are crowded—sometimes intolerably so—into a very limited space, but they are ultimately all alone. Anonymity prevails, and each individual is so highly self-conscious of the boundaries or limits of his or her area of responsibility that community, involving the sharing of burdens, becomes virtually impossible. The more our individuality is defined in terms of our will, our obligations, and our deeds, the more clearly isolated we become one from another. The isolation, plus the tremendous burden of responsibility that goes with voluntarism (to say nothing of the strenuous character of this form of life), have proved too demanding for many people, a fact which expresses itself in highly secularized youth who want to abandon all responsibility for contemporary world problems and attempt instead to form around themselves small communities in which a highly aestheticized form of life is developed.*

TEMPORALISM

Modern secularization takes time very seriously, and not only in the essentially moralistic sense which equates time with the acquisition of wealth. The trait is more fundamental. Time here means primarily the *present* and *immediate* reality which life confronts and through which it moves. Attention is focused on the "here and now" and away from the unchanging, the lasting, or the time-spanning. The temporal, in short, replaces the eternal as the dominant human concern. This trait of secularization reverses a long trend in the history of Western civilization. Although Christianity, following its Hebraic past, placed a high value on time and history, a tendency to "eternalism" manifested itself in the development of Christianity from the time of Au-

* See below, pp. 195–98.

gustine to the Renaissance. Certain doctrines deeply rooted in classical Greek philosophy enhanced this tendency. The true and the good, though they may be glimpsed by beings who exist in an order of time and change, are themselves fixed and unchanging. The Bible refers to the seen things of the present as "temporal" and to the unseen as "eternal." The real is that which somehow transcends time, for time is an order of decay and the science of what is transitory and evanescent.

Secularization reverses the pattern. With the emphasis on the importance of "this" world in space, there has been a corresponding emphasis on the importance of "this" time in the dual sense of the insistent present and the actual course of history. The biological revolution of the last century and the almost fantastic belief in history expressed by Hegel and those thinkers who followed him, served to focus attention on time, change, and development as final facts. The triumph of time over space was further enhanced by two major technological developments—rapid transportation and new and fabulous means of communication. The possibility of experiencing two continents within the hours of one day, and of transmitting, through sound and sight, events taking place on one continent so that men widely separated in space can experience them contemporaneously—these modern miracles have forced upon us an undeniable sense of the *present.* In contrast with the present—the moment of decision and of action—the past seems dull and ineffectual, and even the future, while obviously important, seems too ethereal to merit primary concern. Life is compressed, as it were, into each of its immediate moments and reaches an intensity, almost a frenzy, which expresses itself in what I shall call aestheticism.*

The emphasis on the present alone is the most recent form of temporalism. In a slightly earlier stage of secularization—one whose dominant temper was expressed in pragmatism—the reduction of time to the present had not yet taken place. In that stage time was viewed more concretely and the emphasis was

* See below, pp. 195ff.

placed on the future. The concern was largely directed to what *might* or *could* be accomplished and to the marshalling of past knowledge and of present resources for an attack upon the future. This concern is, of course, still powerful since it accompanies all the other traits of secularization, but temporalism carries the reduction of time further. Now the passion is to be in the present, and that means, in many cases, actually being in the presence of the event as it takes place. We do not want merely to read about the horrors of war, we want to see men die. We do not want merely to hear about the murder "in cold blood," we want it depicted for us in vivid terms which will place us—as fascinated observers, of course—at the scene of the crime as it happens. The concern is ultimately aesthetic; living in the immediate induces us to forget the past and, at least temporarily, to be free from that burdensome responsibility for the future which the autonomous, voluntaristic, secular life demands.

Among the important consequences of temporalism are, first, the loss of interest in long-range projects which require a continuous commitment of loyalty and devotion over an extended period of life and often in the face of disappointment and defeat, and, second, the loss of orientation or aim. Both losses represent the inevitable outcome of conceiving life as essentially a momentary affair. The shift of attention away from "things eternal" and from a divine other world to the things and goods of this world was a move in the direction of taking the world of time, change, and history seriously. But the outworking of temporalism means not only the shift from the eternal to the temporal, but a second shift from the temporal understood as the continuity of past, present, and future to the momentary in which only the present counts. Life is equated with moment-to-moment encounters, a series of episodes each of which is self-enclosed and sufficient to the extent to which they furnish a person with the sense of being "real," that is, the opportunity either for spontaneous self-expression or for experiencing as a spectator some fascinating—usually violent—spectacle. But it is important to notice that moment-to-moment existence taken as the standard of life quite clearly excludes both the extended loyalty needed for sustaining the stabilizing institutions of society and the purposive aim without which individual life can find no enduring satisfaction. For the corporate life of an institution and the purposeful existence of an individual person each requires continuing factors which direct and unify its development. In neither case is the standpoint of temporalism in its radical form adequate, because from that standpoint there is only the present and its isolated experience, and even if there be a series of such presents, the items in the series remain just what they are each in themselves. They do not contribute to a purposive result nor can they be seen as stages in an ongoing life which has an aim. The triumph of time over eternity in secularization ends with the triumph of the present over time itself.

AESTHETICISM

Like the other traits of secularization, aestheticism develops an exaggerated form which must be seen ultimately as the corruption of a response which is both understandable and justifiable in itself. The exaggeration must be understood in contrast with the more normal expression of the trait. As I indicated earlier, I am not entirely happy with the term "aestheticism," because it is vague and open to misunderstanding, but the main features of modern life it is intended to indicate are tolerably clear. Secularization has meant an active and strenuous form of life. And in those Western countries where Protestant Christianity has been powerful, a definite moralism has made itself felt. Moralism means an over-emphasis on duty, on the performance of one's obligations and definite restrictions on the emotions and on spontaneous self-expression which represents the "play" or "relaxation" in an otherwise rigorous existence. I do not mean to open up a full-scale discussion of the frequently repeated charge that Protestantism excluded the arts or destroyed what one writer has called the "aesthetic firmament." The fact is that Protestantism fostered the arts of the "ear"—music, poetry, and rhetoric—which might be called the "rationalistic" arts because of their appeal to significant form which must be grasped in thought. On the other hand, Protestantism tended to neglect the arts of the "eye"—painting, architecture, and the plastic arts—which have often been identified as "art" *par excellence.* The difference involved is by no means unimportant, and it would have a central place in a more extended discussion, but what I am calling aestheticism points to the aesthetic dimension of life which lies beneath the well-formed and highly self-conscious expression exhibited in the identifiable arts starting with the dance and ending with sculpture. Aestheticism is the response to moralism; it is the declaration of man's freedom to enjoy the sensuous part of his nature, over against those who, like the Victorians, officially pronounce it "unclean," or over against the fierce competition for success in modern life which excludes any form of "play" as unprofitable if not actually immoral.

The sexual revolution in secularization illustrates aestheticism very nicely. We have moved from the attitude that human sexual relations were an absolutely private affair not to be brought into the context of public discussion, to the view that these relations can and must be the subject of objective scrutiny and that they are legitimate material for a variety of other forms of public exhibition. Psychological and sociological studies of man's sexual response led the way, and in the course of two decades the most intimate aspects of our sexual encounters have come to be depicted on screen, stage, and in works of fiction to an extent which would not have been believed possible at the end of the last century or even as late as 1940. Along with the development of free public expression has gone a corresponding openness on the part of everyone, not only the young, in thinking and speaking about the problems and potentialities of human passion. The challenge presented by the sexual revolution to much traditional thinking about sex focuses on *freedom* in this most intimate relationship and especially on questioning the belief that sexual intercourse exists only for procreation. Moreover, special attention is now being given to the rights and freedoms of women in the sexual encounter, especially their right to satisfaction often denied in a male-dominated relationship that has tended to reduce the female partner to an object of enjoyment or, in the same fashion, to a source of pleasure to which only the male has a right.

I chose the sexual revolution as an example of aestheticism not because this trait coincides with the sexual dimension of human life, but because it represents in a striking way the expression of the autonomy of feeling and of man as a sensuous animal in the midst of a highly organized, competitive society. Aestheticism expresses itself in many other ways on the modern scene—through all forms of popular art; through unconventional styles of clothing involving bold color, new designs, and a greater exposure of the female form than ever before; through a new concern for gastronomy and refined taste in drinking; through both spectator and active sports; through countless other forms of spontaneous self-expression in singing, dancing, and the theater arts. It is beyond our present scope to attempt to explain how aestheticism intrudes itself into the more enduring and profound art forms, although these forms are by no means captured by this temper. The fact is that serious music, drama, painting, and architecture require a discipline that is not compatible with aestheticism, where the emphasis falls on immediate enjoyment, immediate self-expression, or both. And yet the well-founded and lasting arts can as little afford to ignore the temper of aestheticism as can religion. The proper response of modern art to secularization constitutes a chapter in its own right.

In its extreme form, aestheticism approaches the point of pure self-enjoyment as well as approaching total irresponsibility. All concern for the duties that inevitably go with the maintenance of a free public order is lost, and the sensuous dimension of life is allowed to express itself without restraint. Here temporalism in its extreme form and aestheticism, also in its extreme form, merge. In each case we find the same demand for the immediate, and the tendency to reduce life to a series of "moments" that are charged with high emotional intensity in contrast with which ordinary life seems drab indeed.

The momentous question which faces the religious communities at present is this: What is the proper response to secularization and how shall the religious insights of the tradition be related to this dominant fact about modern life? As with all large questions of this sort, the erroneous answers seem to be easier to arrive at than the correct one. One thing is clear, a simple and undialectical response from either side in relation to the other does not even begin to deal with the real issues. That is to say, the response to secularization from the religious standpoint cannot be that of flat condemnation, nor, on the other hand, will the proponents of secularization be correct in assuming that religion has been superseded entirely because the "secular city" is secure within itself and has no need for religion. We will consider the reasons behind these judgments, but first a word is necessary concerning the much used and abused term, "dialectical." As the term is used here, it has both an existential or ontological reference, and a logical reference. With regard to the first, to say that two forms of life, two outlooks, two ideas, two systems of thought are dialectically related is to say that each is defined in some essential way in relation to the other such that a change in one brings about some corresponding change in the other. Were two distinguishable items wholly externally related, each might change without the change itself effecting any corresponding change in the other. With regard to the logical reference, to say that a question or its answer is "dialectical" means that competing and conflicting claims have to be taken into account, implying that the truth does not rest unambiguously on one side or the other. The flat rejection of secularization as just so much evil and error from the religious standpoint would be an undialectical answer to the question as to how the two are related. Truth would be entirely on the religious side and error wholly on the side of secularization. Similarly, the rejection of religion as totally erroneous from the side of secularization would be an undialectical answer to the question. The truth is that each has relevant and valid criticisms against the other; this implies their dialectical relationship which in turn demands that any proposal for relating them must likewise be dialectical.

There are at least three reasons why secularization cannot be rejected as merely erroneous and therefore evil by the religious traditions. First, secularization represents a logical development from the religious premises of the Judeo-Christian faith. Second, secularization functions as a form of prophetic criticism, laying bare the failure of the churches and of religious people to embody the ideals of their faith and to show its bearing on modern life. Third, religious faith decays if it becomes a merely complacent ornament; that faith must be capable of responding to every challenge, which is precisely what it fails to do in this instance if it turns its back on secularization and abandons the secular city to its own devices.

That secularization in the West represents both a logical and a historical development of religious premises can readily be shown. Of all the religious traditions, the Judeo-Christian is second to none in its positive evaluation of the world of nature, of human individuality, and of the creative order of history. Contrary both to popular suppositions and to the doctrines of some other religions, neither Judaism nor Christianity in its essential teachings rejects the world as evil, or fails to see the creative possibilities in individual personality and in the historical order. In biblical language, the world, man, and time are "creatures" of God, and as such they are declared to be "good." This is not to say that they are not subject to corruption in many ways, but such corruption does not belong to them in virtue of their created status. The world, man, and history are regarded as substantial enough to express both the nature and the will of God. Consequently, they cannot be viewed as in any sense belonging to an order which stands in opposition to God as "matter" or "error" are supposed to do in some religions. Man, moreover, in biblical perspective, is said to have the destiny, under certain conditions, of being "lord" over creation, which implies that his creative development both of the resources of nature and of himself represents an activity in accordance with his own nature. The traits of secularization are in many ways the realization of the destiny both of man and the world, once again, viewed from the standpoint of biblical religion. It is not necessary at this juncture to consider the extent to which evil and corruption have attended this historical development. It is obvious that both have been rampant, but that is not the point. It is of the utmost importance as far as understanding secularization is concerned, to see that *the development itself is not a form of corruption*, but rather that the development is the further expression of the possibilities inherent in creation. The religious response therefore cannot be a bemoaning of the fact of secularization, or a sentimental harking back to some former age of piety that existed prior to man's "fall" into autonomy or before history was transformed into a purely secular order. The Western religious tradition spawned secularization; the task of those who still adhere to that tradition is to understand and to judge the results of secularization with insight derived from religious faith. This task is something very different from supposing that the proper religious assessment of secularization is the judgment that it should never have happened in the first place.

The second reason supporting the claim that secularization should not be flatly rejected from the religious standpoint is found in the prophetic function which secularization performs in exploring the shortcomings and failures of the religious institutions. In many respects, secularization taken as a total phenomenon represents the critical or prophetic voice which the religious institutions were either unable or unwilling to raise against themselves. There are three principal shortcomings revealed, and the different churches within Christianity share the responsibility for them jointly, even if somewhat unevenly as regards a given breach of responsibility. Secularization reveals, first, that the churches failed to keep pace with modern thought and the changing institutions of modern life, and, for the most part, failed to reinterpret their religious insights in terms intelligible to the modern man; second, that there has been a continued use of ecclesiastical authority for establishing religious beliefs and practices, implying a lack of faith in experience and understanding as means of persuasion, and a corresponding lack of regard for individual conscience; third, that there has been widespread failure on the part of Christians to guide and shape modern society in accordance with the norms of Christian morality.

The secularized man, regardless of any critical judgment that may come to be made upon his own style of life, is correct in exposing these failures stemming from individual Christians and Christian institutions alike. Too often Christianity through its spokesmen has resisted the advance of science and has refused to examine its sacred doctrines in the light of new knowledge and novel patterns of thought. While the modern man has been taught through his secular education to think in twentieth-century psychological, sociological, and economic terms, the churches have frequently continued to think in patterns derived from the nineteenth century, if not much earlier. The churches have often supported racial prejudices that stand in flat contradiction to their professed moral code, and in many instances they have refused to join with any fervor in the fight against social and economic injustice. Moreover, the churches, both Catholic and Protestant, have misread the meaning of the modern man's drive toward autonomy of thought and conscience; instead of seeking to engage him through intelligent reinterpretation of faith which appeals to his understanding and his experience, they have resorted instead to older forms of authoritarianism which may coerce but do not convince. Finally, the churches have often been complacent, depending for support on the conventional sanctions for religion—respectability, ignorance, and superstition—instead of seeking new foundations for faith in a society which increasingly channels into secular pursuits the energy that formerly went into religion.

The third reason why secularization cannot be condemned out of hand from the religious standpoint is that the Judeo-Christian tradition cannot consistently abandon its concern for and involvement in the "world." To leave secularization to its own devices on the ground that it is hopelessly wrong, confused, irresponsible, and guilty of other moral lapses, would itself be a monstrous display of irresponsibility on the part of the spokesmen for religion. For the fact is that secularization, regardless of the truth it represents, is not an unmixed blessing. The secular man is still in need of a truth which the religious perspective contains and which his secular creed does not teach. That truth is that man, left with no limit or standard beyond himself, inevitably loses his humility, absolutizes his own perspective, and ends in a frenzy of self-conceit from which he is unable to escape by further acts of will. The point is not that man's autonomy should be denied or nullified, but rather that the dialectical character of autonomy needs to be made clear, and this can be done only from a perspective that is beyond man. The task, therefore, of those who uphold the religious perspective is to make clear the extent to which secularization runs the risk of losing the very autonomy it holds so dear because of its own loss of a self-critical perspective.

Insofar as the churches were either unwilling or unable to develop forms of self-criticism, the lessons of these failures will have to be learned from the secularization which raises itself as a prophetic voice. The secular domain is not merely the other or the "enemy" standing over against the religious; on the contrary, it forms a proving ground in and through which the consistency of faith with practice is brought to the test. Religion is therefore internally connected with the very secularization which it helped to produce and which now confronts it with a critical eye and an accusing finger. If, therefore, secularization is condemned from the religious standpoint this can only mean that the spokesmen for religion have failed to appreciate both the truth in the criticism and their responsibility for having made it necessary.

Since the response to secularization from the religious standpoint cannot be that of rejection or flat condemnation, what then is the proper response? On the positive side, one point is clear: the response cannot be a capitulation either. The spokesmen for religion cannot simply abandon their faith and accept secularization as the final truth about life. The proper response from the religious communities entails their pointing out the *limits* of secularization and the self-destructive excesses which stem from man's failure to acknowledge his own limitations. The insight which the religious perspective brings is that man inevitably misuses his freedom and thus falls prey to some form of corruption regardless of the direction in which he seeks to realize himself. Thus, although each of the traits of secularization expresses a legitimate potentiality in man and in the society he creates, each is subject to a corruptive excess stemming from man's loss of humility and unwillingness to acknowledge his own limitations. Autonomy itself runs to excess and the result is the formless freedom of the existential man whose freedom cannot attain an overarching purpose or direction without ceasing to be freedom. Similarly, all the other traits of secularization run to an excess which is either actually or potentially self-destructive. Technology reaches the point where it destroys the natural world it was intended to develop; voluntarism ends in an utter individualism which destroys community and thus paralyzes each isolated individual and deprives him of every form of co-operation and loyalty through which his will can be realized; temporalism ends with a concern for the moment so intense that life is dissolved into unrelated episodes through which no integrated self is possible and no self-fulfillment can be attained; aestheticism ends with irresponsible self-expression that cannot be other than parasitic since the free institutions of modern life can be sustained only by the acceptance of public responsibility on the part of every citizen.

What the religious insight into the corruption of freedom brings is not a total judgment on secularization as an historical development which takes place apart from human thought and will, but rather a judgment on man himself. It is man and not an impersonal development known as "secularization" which is at fault, just as it is man and not "religion" which is at fault on the other side. The failures of religion which produced secularization, and the destructive tendencies in secularization itself, both stem from the fact that man misuses his freedom. The difference is that this fact is known from the religious perspective even if men of faith have not often enough understood the extent to which it applies to themselves.

The urgent question now is: How can the judgment which is rightly made by religion on secularization be brought to bear in the present situation? The answer is that it must be made with humility and indirectly through what has come to be called the "religionless" religion. The religious insight cannot be enforced by the authority of positive religion. We have seen the great harm caused by that approach. Instead, the insight must be proclaimed "unofficially," in a way that appeals to man's experience and his understanding. The religious truth must be asserted by religious people as the truth, and not merely as a vested interest of an institution or a church. The proper perspective can be attained if men of faith understand the religious dimension of experience and see that the judgment it brings can be effective only if made in a non-dogmatic way—in a way, that is, which is free of the authoritarianism, the self-righteousness, and the condescension which have been associated with "religion" in the past. Religious insight is forced to come in a "religionless" form because the egregious failures of religious people and institutions in the modern world have led the secular man to distrust whatever is associated with "religion." This does not mean that positive religion should disappear, because religion loses its life when it no longer has the structure provided by worship and the celebration of the Holy. On the contrary, the idea of the "religionless" religion means the formation of a new consciousness on the part of the representatives of positive religion. This new consciousness requires the acknowledgment that the religious judgment on man and his misuse of freedom applies to *all* men, including, or especially, those who mediate that judgment in the world.

The encounter at present between religion and secularization can be a creative one if each side sees the truth in the criticism of the other. Secularization exposes the tendency to corruption in the authority of positive religion and the failure of both individuals and churches to embody the religious ideals in the world. The insight of religion exposes man's misuse of freedom in secularization and the tendency of man to absolutize his own perspective. A positive result can be achieved if each side grasps and appropriates the insight that without self-criticism no lasting form of human life is possible—sacred or secular.

Index

aestheticism, 181, 195ff
Amos, 88
Anselm of Canterbury, 94, 122ff, 129, 155, 176n
anthropological argument. *See* argument
Aquinas, St. Thomas, 4-5, 93, 116, 134, 140
argument, 101, 107, 121ff, 126ff, 132
  anthropological, 149ff
  cosmological, 81, 90, 133ff, 137
  ontological, 81, 121ff, 134, 137
  teleological, 134, 145ff
argumentation, 101-2
Aristotle, 4, 21-2, 115
Atman, 176-7
Augustine of Hippo, 4-6, 94, 108, 114, 135, 169, 192
autonomy, 183ff

B

Barth, Karl, 94
Being, 11, 19, 64, 75, 102n, 122, 143
Bernard, St., 94
Bonaventure, St., 149n
Buddha, 173, 177-8
Buddhism, 8, 16, 41, 74, 164, 168, 176-7

C

celebration, 57–8, 62, 76, 205
Christ, Jesus, 68, 73, 76, 78-9, 80, 85, 87-8, 92-3, 143, 143n, 144, 170-71, 173
Christianity, 8-10, 16, 65, 68, 77, 80-81, 94, 97, 108, 110, 164, 168, 170–71, 175–76, 192, 195, 199
community:
  of anticipation, 80, 92
  of memory, 80
  religious, 17-18, 20, 70, 72, 76, 96, 158ff
  scientific, 161ff
cosmological arguments. *See* argument

D

deliverer, 166-8, 172-4, 175ff
Descartes, René, 137
Dewey, John, 21, 22, 51, 115
disclosure. *See* revelation
doubt, 99ff
  and incongruity, 103ff

E

Empiricism:
  British, 26
  radical, 12

encounter, 7, 12-16, 24ff, 30-31, 33-6, 38, 41ff, 49, 51, 72, 77, 84f, 92–3, 96, 128, 132, 205
rational, 132n
See also experience
events, 27, 45
crucial, 58-9, 62ff, 66, 76
existence, 6, 15, 44n, 54, 118, 125ff, 138
existentialism, 6
experience, 11-14, 18, 21ff, 124, 152ff
as activity, 27
dimensions of, 36ff
as "given," 22, 25
immediate, 52f, 81ff
interpreted, 52ff
as "mental," 24ff, 29, 34-6
moral dimension of, 22
pure, 14
religious, 11, 46ff, 51, 55
religious dimension of, 9, 15-17, 46ff, 55ff, 63ff, 75f, 165
sense, 22, 26-8, 52, 119
shared, 163ff
social character of, 30-31
theory of, 21-2, 28-9, 53
as triadic, 35
expression, 12, 23, 41ff, 71n. *See also* Language

F

fact, 39-40
faith, 20, 54, 63, 75, 95, 102, 103, 107, 110, 117n, 155, 199
freedom, 181, 183ff, 189n

G

God, 3, 5-6, 11, 14, 18-19, 37, 41, 48n, 57, 105ff, 184, 199
the Absolutely Exalted, 122ff, 130ff, 150f, 157
concept of, 65, 123ff, 127
disclosure of, 68ff
existence of, 15, 51f, 81f, 90, 100, 108
idea of, 19, 46ff, 63ff
as name, 65, 75
presence of, 52, 76, 79, 83, 90, 91, 155-6
problem of, 15-17, 19, 65
reality of, 108ff, 111, 118f, 133
result of inference, 52ff, 81ff, 110, 141
guilt, 19, 48, 93, 163

H

Hartshorne, Charles, 94
Hegel, G. W. F., 193
Hinduism, 164, 168
history, 37, 45, 181, 193, 199, 200
patterns in, 89ff
Hocking, W. E., 114n
holy, 56ff, 63, 75, 97, 187, 205
Hume, David, 21

I

ideal, 169ff
individualism, 181, 185, 190ff
intelligibility, 115ff, 121, 131, 133, 136, 137n, 138, 155
interpretation, 14, 20, 49ff, 74, 86, 87, 99
philosophical, 50
Isaiah, 73, 77, 88, 91, 170
Islam, 10, 16, 145, 164

J

James, William, 21, 46, 47, 52
Jeremiah, 77
Job, 90ff, 105f, 169
Joseph legend, 160
Judaism, 16, 163

K

Kant, Immanuel, 12, 42, 114n, 118, 125, 127, 133n, 134, 136n, 137, 147ff, 150, 183, 184, 185, 186
Kierkegaard, Søren, 117, 155

L

language, 6-7, 13, 23, 41f, 45, 52, 69, 86, 132. *See also* expression
of history, 45
of logic, 44n
ordinary, 43ff
of science, 43

Law, Old Testament, 88
Leibniz, G. W. F., 137
"linguistic turn," 41ff
Locke, John, 21-2, 183
logic, 22, 43, 117, 132
  language of, 44n
Logos, 19, 94, 95
love, 110, 122, 173
Luther, Martin, 94

M

mediation, 52f, 88. *See also* revelation, medium (media) of
Mohammed, 144
Moral argument, 81
Moses, 73, 76, 78, 88, 143, 143n, 144

N

need, 171ff
Nirvana, 177
nominalism, 9, 18

O

occasions, historical, 19, 70, 81, 83, 89
  general, 19, 143n
  special, 72ff, 143n
ontological argument. *See* argument

P

Paul, St., 73, 87, 143, 160-61
Peirce, Charles Sanders, 21, 101, 101n, 114, 118, 119
Plato, 6
Plotinus, 81
profane, 57ff, 75, 180. *See also* secular
prophet, 87f, 170
Protestantism, 17, 192
purpose, 54, 85, 158

R

realism, 25
reason:
  formal, 111ff
  living, 111ff
relations, 23, 37, 38
religion, 8, 13, 22, 46ff, 61, 203
  comparative, 164f
  and doubt, 103ff
  Hebraic, 88f
  natural, 96
  positive, 15, 19, 75-6, 95, 97
  as relation, 47, 49, 82, 110ff
  "religionless," 204–5
  and secularization, 180ff
religious object, 48ff, 48n, 66, 109, 159, 166ff
revelation, 19, 49ff, 66f, 68ff, 124
  medium (media) of, 68ff, 71n, 77f, 80
  paradox of, 98ff
Rousseau, Jean Jacques, 183
Royce, Josiah, 97-8, 150n
Russell, Bertrand, 44n, 137, 137n

S

sacred, 57, 201. *See also* holy
science, 22, 39-40, 43, 47, 53, 54, 111, 116, 161ff, 188
secular, 4, 57ff, 180f, 201. *See also* profane
secularization, 180ff
self, 31-2, 34, 36, 49, 84ff, 93ff, 103, 104, 114ff, 131, 159, 184–5, 191
  individual, 32, 46, 112ff, 152f, 186
  as selective interest, 31
sexual revolution, 196f
signs, 86, 91
structure, 11, 23, 25, 165ff, 191

T

technology, 187ff, 203
teleological argument. *See* argument
temporalism, 192ff, 203
theology, 5-8
Tillich, Paul, 94, 116n, 119, 119n, 185

V

Vedanta, 176, 178
voluntarism, 182n, 190ff, 203

W

Whitehead, Alfred North, 6, 143n, 177